T0339506

The Politics of Organizational Change

Politics is an aspect of everyday life within organizations, and is a force that inhibits individual and collective behaviour. If not fully understood, it can impede organizational change and development. In order to minimise the political aspects of organizational dynamics there is a need to understand the extent to which organizational culture brings about politicised conformance and how individuals shape their behaviour through self-interest to conform—sense-giving and sense-making nexus—thus moderating the degree of change initiatives.

The Politics of Organizational Change explores the relationship between self-interest, power, politics and managing organizational change from a theoretical perspective. It encourages the fundamental questioning of the relationship between self-interest, power and control inherent within organizational change, and discusses the attendant implications for managing change. It will be of value to those who require a text that goes beyond set patterns of coverage found in textbooks dealing with managing change.

Robert Price is Senior Lecturer in Organizational Change Management and Leadership at Suffolk Business School, University of Suffolk (UK), and is Chair of the Organizational Studies Track, British Academy of Management.

Routledge Focus on Business and Management

The fields of business and management have grown exponentially as areas of research and education. This growth presents challenges for readers trying to keep up with the latest important insights. Routledge Focus on Business and Management presents small books on big topics and how they intersect with the world of business research.

Individually, each title in the series provides coverage of a key academic topic, whilst collectively, the series forms a comprehensive collection across the business disciplines.

The Neuroscience of Rhetoric in Management
Compassionate Executive Communication
Dirk Remley

Heidegger and Entrepreneurship
A Phenomenological Approach
Håvard Åsvoll

The Politics of Organizational Change
Robert Price

Globalization And Entrepreneurship In Small Countries
Mirjana Radović – Marković and Rajko Tomaš

The Business of New Process Diffusion
Management of the Early Float Glass Start-ups
Brychan Celfyn Thomas and Alun Merlyn Thomas

For more information about this series, please visit: www.routledge.com/
Routledge-Focus-on-Business-and-Management/book-series/FBM

The Politics of Organizational Change

Robert Price

Routledge
Taylor & Francis Group

NEW YORK AND LONDON

First published 2019
by Routledge
605 Third Avenue, New York, NY 10017

and by Routledge
2 Park Square, Milton Park, Abingdon, Oxon, OX14 4RN

First issued in paperback 2021

Routledge is an imprint of the Taylor & Francis Group, an informa business

Library of Congress Cataloging-in-Publication Data
Names. Price, Robert Huw, 1961– author.
Title: The politics of organizational change / Robert Price.
Description: New York : Routledge, 2019. | Series: Routledge focus
  on business and management | Includes index.
Identifiers: LCCN 2019006989 | ISBN 9781138605794 (hardback) |
  ISBN 9780429467950 (ebook)
Subjects: LCSH: Organizational change. | Management.
Classification: LCC HD58.8 .P7385 2019 | DDC 658.4/06—dc23
LC record available at https://lccn.loc.gov/2019006989

ISBN 13: 978-1-03-224121-0 (pbk)
ISBN 13: 978-1-138-60579-4 (hbk)

DOI: 10.4324/9780429467950

Typeset in Times New Roman
by Apex CoVantage, LLC

Contents

Acknowledgements

I am grateful to a number of friends and colleagues who, over the years, have listened to my views on self-interest and politicised conformance, and who have encouraged, and in some cases cajoled, me to put my thoughts into words. If it were not for their forbearance and encouragement, I would not have written this book—I thank you.

Preface

This book, at least in one sense, is covering the well-trod ground of organizational politics; however, and this is where the book deviates from the path, it seeks to discuss organizational politics from a perspective which focuses on the role and power of self-interest in shaping individual and others' political behaviour, generally, and in relation to organizational change. With this in mind, my desire is that it is not seen as just another book dealing with organizational politics found on the well-trod path. Therefore, this book is for those "travellers" that wish to explore an aspect of change that is rarely openly discussed, that is, self-interest in relation to concentric circles of self and how this shapes attitude and behaviour to, and as part of, change in relation to those that are close or distant to self.

The discussion places individuals at the very centre of political dynamics as part of change, and does so in order to attempt to repurpose the debate surrounding the sources and impact of organizational politics, and not to see politics as a force that, in a simplistic sense, emanates entirely from what organizations through others do to us. The premise is one where organizational politics is something that *we* do to ourselves, to others and in relation to organization. It is an attribute we take into work, it is part of us; it is, in one sense, unavoidable! We tend to ascribe political behaviour to others, but not to ourselves—the self invariably perceived as either being non-political, or at the very least, we are not as political as others are, with oneself being more politically pure and distanced and/or exempt from the political milieu. Therefore, I felt it was time for a discussion that focuses on how and why individuals behave politically based on self-interest: seeing self-interest as a powerful constraining force determined by, and through, individual actions and reactions to change. A dynamic force that shapes the degree to which individuals participate in change; and how politicised behaviour shapes dynamics beyond what is recognised and discussed within organizations, generally, and as part of organizational change. It is a known force, but rarely openly discussed; it is, to all intents and purpose, the "*power that dare not speak its name*".

In addition, after a good number of years teaching managing organizational change to undergraduate and postgraduate students, I became increasingly dissatisfied with the well-trod path, albeit a path that provides a rounded view of organizational politics; but a path that does not provide, at least for me, a deeper more nuanced exploration of organizational politics, self-interest, conformance and change. The discussion of self-interest is, of course, not new, but placing self-interest at the centre of organizational politics in relation to change is a different starting point, and is done so to better understand individual behaviour as part of change beyond, perhaps, making assumptions about the efficacy of change management processes that are participative in orientation. One element of the managing change mantra is to put individuals at the centre of change in order for change to become embedded through individuals' attitude and behaviour to the new; however, the element that is invariably missing is the degree to which self-interest has centrality in the power dynamic inherent within change, and how this shapes attitude and behaviour. A power dynamic that enables employees, either individually and/or collectively, to exercise power to maintain individual agenda in relation to organizational change agenda.

In order to understand the power of self-interest and the extent to which it drives organizational political behaviour in relation to change, and to capture the relationship between individuals and organization, I decided to base the discussion on the concept and action of *proskynesis* in relation to concentric circles of self. *Proskynesis* is the act of kissing towards, or bowing and/or prostrating oneself before individuals of a higher social status; in terms of organization, I see it as the relationship between positional power through hierarchy and structure. I use *proskyneis* as the embodiment of organizational politics, especially in relation to why individuals metaphorically "bow" and/or "prostrate" themselves through politicised conformance as a way of demonstrating recognition of where power through hierarchy lies. For many, to question the role and power of self-interest will be anathema to what modern organization is supposed to represent with regard to the degree to which individuals are valued, respected and placed at the centre of organizational performance. Modern organizational management narratives imply relationships and organizational forms that are akin to a form of pantisocracy; however, organizations through structure and hierarchy are more akin to clerisy based on individuals knowing their position and which manifests itself through political behaviour. I therefore decided to take a path less well known and one that significantly deviates in order to take the reader in a different direction. A direction that encourages the reader to question a number of things about the role that self-interest plays in organizational change, and how, paradoxically, its inherent power increases organizational control, yet at the same time reduces it.

The book's structure is one that takes the reader along a path that meanders, that is, from a start point of philosophical interpretation of self-interest through to managing the political and power dynamic of change—or at least attempting to manage through it! The book's pathway presents the reader with a number of distinct but inter-related strands that weft and weave in order to facilitate a more nuanced discussion and understanding of self-interest based political behaviour, and thus power through conformance. The five chapters cover a number of inter-related aspects, from the roots of self-interest through to attempting to *manage the unmanageable* (a deliberate oxymoron!) based on non-rhetorical action. Chapter 1 discusses the root of self-interest, locus of power, politicised behaviour and maintaining position through politicised behaviour. Chapter 2 develops the themes by covering organizational and individual change narratives, the concept of mutually assured delusions and politicised behaviour, and "white space" and political behaviour. Chapter 3 discusses power through politics and control, the politics of resistance and political aspects of psychological contracts. Chapter 4 develops the first three chapters in relation to the implications of the politics of change: realpolitik; illusion of control; politics power and control; and rational-emotional response to change. Chapter 5 focuses on "managing the unmanageable", antithesis of political behaviour and the power of, and need for, action beyond rhetoric in order to try to shape the political dynamics of change.

Moreover, the book aims to provide not only insights into the ways in which organizational political behaviour based on self-interest manifests itself, but to re-energise the debate of the role it plays within politicised conformance and concomitant power dynamics as part of organizational change. In addition, it is not intended that the book replace or subvert extant interpretations and understanding of organizational politics; however, the book is intended to add a layer to our understanding of self-interest and politicised conformance. A layer that is not only more nuanced but also more realistic in terms of the power of self-interest and the extent to which, alongside other factors, it shapes attitude and behaviour at work, both generally and within change.

Throughout the book, I use "individual" and "employees" synonymously in order to avoid repetition of a single word. I trust this will be forgiven, and make the book easier to read.

Introduction

The purpose of this book is to explore the relationship between self-interest, power, politics and managing organizational change, and to do so in relation to individuals' perception of self relative to what change means to, and requires of, them—this places individuals at the centre of change in a highly personalised and subjective sense. Recognising and understanding the centrality of self-interest as a powerful motivating force, and understanding it as part of the milieu of managing change, helps us understand how it determines individual choices and actions, in an externalised and internalised behaviour sense, with regard to accepting the degree to which individuals may resist proposed changes. This is not to suggest that self-interest can be managed, but by understanding its centrality in shaping how individuals perceive, interpret and react to change may provide a more nuanced understanding of the limits to organizational control, generally, and in relation to change. Politicised behaviour, based on self-interest, manifests itself in many forms; therefore, there is also a need to understand the bases of self-interest in order to consider the degree to which it shapes resistance to change, and the extent to which self-interest needs to have more prominence within change management frameworks.

Next, I shall start by making a firm, and some would say rash, controversial and erroneous statement, which is, *if senior management decides that change is required then irrespective of the approach used, change will happen.* For many, this statement will very much go against the grain of how to manage change and will be viewed as heterodox as it fundamentally challenges the precepts of change through participative dialogical approaches. I do not, however, seek to undermine the overall validity and efficacy of such approaches, but to place self-interest politicised conformance and its inherent power more central to our understanding of the forces that bring about change; forces that do not necessarily reside within the control of organizations and appointed change agents. In the main, most organizational change textbooks propagate the view that meaningful and deeper change is achieved through participative approaches, especially, albeit in a simplistic sense, in relation of the adage that imposed change is invariably opposed. This supports the view that change through participation and dialogue engenders a more open attitude and preparedness to change, and is more deeply embedded, though ideally, not in a "refreeze" sense. A counter to this well-worn adage is that what is invariably missing is a recognition of the degree to which individuals behave in a self-interested way, generally, and through their dialogue with those individuals tasked with managing change on a day-to-day basis when change is underway. Therefore, irrespective of the method used to bring about change, individuals behave politically, which shapes the degree and depth of change at individual and collective levels. In addition, and given the number of books, journal articles and "how to" guides etc., which do not discuss self-interest politicised conformance, there is a need to explore self-interest in terms of the degree to which it (1) shapes employee behaviour, (2) shapes individual acceptance of organizational change agenda and (3) the extent to which change is managed beyond that which individuals choose to allow.

Self-interest, more often than not, is an aspect of organizational change ignored or subsumed in a superficial way within book chapters. It is, in one sense, a footnote to managing change, perhaps due to self-interest based politicised conformance not readily fitting a change mantra that generally emphasises the importance of high levels of employee participation in order to manage change well, and especially if transformational change is an end goal. Perhaps, self-interest is not part of change frameworks because it is an aspect of change that is beyond managing, except by individuals themselves—this provides individuals with a significant amount of power and control based on how they decide to shape their response in relation to how managers try to shape them to conform to change requirements. Furthermore, self-interest and how it shapes attitude and behaviour is an aspect of human nature from which we shy away. It is a form of behaviour generally seen as negative and dysfunctional; however, it is a form of behaviour that allows individuals to fit into their social and work environments, in fact, it is essential for being part of a group, society and organization. In addition, it is a form of behaviour that does not conform to societal and organizational norms and expectations—norms and expectations that emphasise and laud rational decision-making driven by collective goals, and not, therefore, about individual agenda.

This view of self-interest, combined with it being beyond the control of management, has shaped the creation and content of change frameworks that focus, quite understandably, on those aspects believed to be within the control of those tasked with managing others through change; self-interest has to a very large degree been "airbrushed" out of managing change history!

Also, it is, perhaps, easier to ignore self-interest, to pretend that it does not exist; it being easier to live in an organizational world that is unitary, rational and devoid of self-interest, all of which, I shall argue, is a delusion. It also removes one aspect of complexity inherent within managing change.

In order to capture the inherent complex relationship between self-interest, conformance and change, the central theme of the book is the performance of proskynesis (Taylor, 1927), which, at least for me, encapsulates the relationship between self-interest and politicised conformance behaviour within organizations. It is politicised conformance through proskynesis and its inherent self-administered control that provides organizations with increased power and control through change, which, at the same time, is a reflection of organizational holding environments and the degree to which they nurture degrees of conformance; a conformance that is in turn reflected through individual agenda. Plato was the first to use the word in written form, and did so in relation to the politics of the Persian Court. Proskynesis required diplomats and courtiers to perform ritualised bowing as a demonstration of recognising the "seat of power" and that individuals were demonstrating conformance to expectations as part of ritual, which if not observed would marginalise individuals to such a degree that they became of no consequence and therefore had no power. Individuals, in order to have place, quickly learnt appropriate behaviour associated with proskynesis. One aspect, however, which had to be learnt very quickly, but not openly discussed, was power through ritualised conformance as a key element of proskynesis—it was expected, if not demanded as a political requirement through a physical act; self-interest dictated that individuals, irrespective of what they really thought, would conform, it became in one sense, a delusory dance. Proskynesis became a ritualised way of conforming to an expected norm in order to be accepted, recognised and to achieve promotion, and, of course, to affect diplomacy, which is synonymous with organizational politics. Employees learn political behaviour as way to fit in, which is a form of proskynesis that creates an illusion of unity through concealment of the true politicised self, irrespective of prevailing organizational culture and approaches used to manage change.

One example from ancient history that demonstrates how proskynesis became an imposed norm outside of the Persian Court, with failure of compliance carrying penalties for non-conformance, is the fate of Callisthenes (360–326 BC). Callisthenes was executed for refusing to bow to Alexander the Great. He viewed Alexander the Great as a mere mortal whom did not have the right to expect subservience; but Alexander believed that as he was the "great leader" he had a paramount position of dominance that deserved to be recognised through a form of proskynesis. By dint of ignoring to play the political game through deference to the seat of ultimate power,

Callisthenes was demonstrating independence and therefore not conforming politically. Some would see this as either a brave or a foolish stance, a stance accompanied by the ultimate sacrifice (cost). Non-conformance within modern organizations is not, of course, subject to execution, but does bring about isolation from an organization's mainstream and, for example, promotion opportunities; and in relation to change, non-conformance to a change agenda is a metaphorical non-bowing, therefore, individuals learn to "bow" to the required changes—a delusion is created through metaphorical bowing. However, this does not preclude individuals changing in line with organizational agenda in a non-politicised way; therefore, for individuals to avoid a form of "organizational death", individuals learn to conform politically in order to survive and/or thrive.

The way in which I use the word "self-interest" throughout this book and how I relate it to proskynesis, is part-based on the 2nd-century stoic philosopher, Hierocles. Hierocles argued that individuals place themselves in relation to proximity to others; connectedness through a series of concentric circles: the human mind (self), immediate family (close colleagues in the work sense), extended family (work colleagues), local community (department or equivalent), community of neighbouring towns (other departments or equivalent), country (organization) and human race (all other stakeholding groups). To clarify things at this point, Hierocles argued that individuals need to draw all the circles into the centre (self) in order to make everyone our concern in order to live a good ethical life. The extent, of course, to which this is possible through life generally and in terms of organization depends on the extent to which an individual can divorce self-interest from thoughts and action in relation to others' lives and attendant needs/requirements/ sense of belonging etc. For individuals to remove self-interest from thoughts and actions in a Hieroclean sense, or at best to minimise it, individuals would be required to subsume self-interested needs to societal (organizational) needs, and do so in a unitary way that is demonstrable through thought, words and actions. Such sublimation can be equated to organizational life, that is, in terms of working together based on mutual concern, respect and working in harmony in order to achieve superordinate goals; however, the extent to which this happens at work, never mind society generally is, of course, open to question. Pinker (2002, p168) when discussing the developmental benefits of co-operation and exchange between individuals, and as an element of society in order to avoid conflict and/or other deprivations, says that individuals form "circles of allies and trading partners" in order to achieve mutually beneficial goals. When looking at organizations as a reflection of society, a microcosm, such behaviour takes place at work, both through forced (dominant) networks based around structure and systems, and through informal networks—a space that facilitates the creation of circles of political allies through trading mutual benefits obtained through collective action within liminal space. The premise of the practice of a form of proskynesis related to self being predominant, though not dominant, at the centre of our self-awareness at work is central to the direction in which I take my discussion. This is not to paint a bleak picture of individuals and organizational life as wholly self-centred; the book does not set out to do this. The discussion is one that tries to make us all think about self-interest and how, even if unspoken, it plays a more significant part in organizational life in relation to change than we are prepared to openly admit and discuss.

Specifically in terms of change, employees thinking in self-interested terms creates a rationale-emotional paradox within individuals as to how to respond and deal with organizational change, that is, what is the right thing to do in terms of organizational requirements set against one's values, norms and view of proposed changes? This in turn requires individuals to decide whether to find their "voice" and, for example, argue against and/or resist aspects of proposed changes. Arguing against and/or resistance may, of course, carry attendant risks associated with "putting one's political head above the political parapet" through not conforming—not playing the proskynesis game. Alternatively, individuals may internalise disagreement and adopt politicised behaviour in order to conform—again, playing the poskynesis game. If disagreement is internalised, it means that organizations are tapping, albeit in an unmanaged and unstructured way, a form of power based on employee self-interest through conformance. A concomitant aspect to self-interest based political conformance is the extent to which liminal spaces created by and through organizational change allow individuals to manoeuvre, dominate and manipulate their space and/or that of others. In addition, individuals, through politicised conformance, are able to demonstrate appropriate behaviour in order to signal going along with change, with such signalling carrying political prizes.

Power based on a form of proskynesis drives change, but does so in a mechanistic and self-control oriented way, in that, control is not only effected through extant hierarchical power, but also by and through individuals agenda in relation to self-interest. It is a form of power that is recognised in relation to self, which in turn reinforces inherent political power that organizations have—it becomes a continuous self-fulfilling prophecy; a prophecy that maintains organizational narratives of "we are/have changed, and everyone is moving in the same direction". This view, specifically, if accepted, fundamentally challenges the degree to which dialogical approaches to managing change are effective in terms of depth. It is, to say the least, difficult to differentiate between the efficacies of such approaches in relation to the degree to which politicised conformance drives change. There is a need, therefore, to consider the basis of how organizational politics affects and shapes change through individuals' attitudes and behaviour, that is, the Hieroclean innermost circle, but with self-centredness dominating individual thought and action manifest through politicised conformance—proskynesis.

References

Pinker, S. (2002) *The Blank Slate*. London: Penguin Books.
Taylor, L. (1927) The "Proskynesis" and the Hellenistic Ruler Cult. *The Journal of Hellenic Studies*, 47, 53–62.

1 Self-Interest and Political Behaviour

This chapter discusses how we learn and develop politicised behaviour at work, in that it is experiential, reflexive and reflective in nature. Individuals within organizations learn through the shaping forces that exist within extant and developing networks, for example, through stories told by colleagues, memes, interpretation and interpolation, general and specific discourse, transmission chains, tone set by active constructors, actors and actants. The learning process of organizational politics also helps individuals to identify specific political behaviour that is associated with positive and/or negative attendant consequences, which is a key part of the learning process that enables individuals to "fit" perceived organizational politicised requirements. Individuals identify, and in a broad sense accept political norms—a form of acculturation takes place within work environments. Bolman and Deal (1997, p163) put forward that organizational politics relates to five elements: (1) coalitions of individuals and interest groups, (2) existence of differences between members, (3) most important decisions relate to scarce resources, (4) power is the most important resource, (5) goals and decisions come through bargaining, negotiation etc. The elements relate to strategic decision-making; however, there is a recognition across all five elements that individuals pursue their own agenda, and do so based on degrees of self-interest or, perhaps at best, enlightened self-interest. Irrespective of how one may view the reasoning behind individual or actions of coalitions, self-interest is present to a lesser or greater degree, and is determined and controlled by individuals through self-control, and, it should be recognised, by key actors with personal leadership power.

Before further discussion, it is necessary to define self-interest in order that there is clarity and consistency in the way it relates to organizational politics and change. In a broad sense, self-interest covers advantage to self when making and taking decisions; it may include egoism, materialism and rationality, and encompasses forms of enlightened self-interest. Following on from this, and for the purpose of this book, *The Routledge Encyclopaedia of Philosophy* (1998) definition is used. "[W]hat is in a person's interests, to well-being" and also relates to: ". . . a motive or disposition of character: persons are said to act from self-interest when they aim at their own good or to be self-interested when they are disposed to pursue their own good".

The definition also highlights that "individuals' identities are constituted by a variety of roles, relations and commitments, and in different institutional contexts under different descriptions individuals can have distinct and sometimes conflicting conceptions of their interests" (O'Neill, 2001). O'Neill's definition is pertinent to the core theme of the discussion throughout this book, in that it highlights the inherent conflict that resides within individuals when considering the way in which they consciously orient their political behaviour and inherent decisions about the degree to which they conform in terms of political behaviour. An individual's politicised behaviour orientation, however, is not fixed; context and changes to context will determine the form it takes—it is a controlled malleable force within self. The other aspect to this is the degree to which self-interest shapes individual agenda in relation to organizational goals. As Cyert and March (1963) highlighted, "Organizations do not have objectives, people do". Individual objectives in relation to organizational objectives require individuals to, depending on agenda, perform proskynesis, but the performance is one that is owned and largely controlled by individuals. However, there is duality of control through self and self-determinate orientation in relation to organizational line management through hierarchy, which manifests itself through degrees of control and power given to organizations through individual and collective politicised conformance. Chapter 2 will explore this aspect further.

The concept of self-interest, even though political aspects are not specifically referred to, can be summarised through Balogun and Hope Hailey's (2004, p149) iteration of Beckhard Harris' (1987) "Change Equation", which identifies three key components of individual reaction to change. The three elements, relative to the nature of change and its impact on individuals, are: (1) the degree to which an individual is satisfied/dissatisfied with the current state, (2) the degree to which the change is desirable, (3) whether or not change is practical. Individuals relate the three elements directly to the perceived cost to self. The degree of cost may then manifest itself in degrees of resistance, whether overt and/or covert. This is not necessarily a binary choice, but nuanced through politicised conformance behaviour: individuals will determine their degree of resistance in relation to the importance they attach to those aspects of the required change that disrupts their satisfaction with the current state. This process takes place irrespective of the change approach used; it is an inescapable aspect of the reality of individual reaction to change measured in terms of "what does it mean for me?"

This also equates to Lewin's (1951) Field Theory in terms of hostility to change that is within the "restraining forces" field; the idea being, of course, to identify the forces that may create resistance to the forces driving change. Lewin's Field Theory has been criticised for being a top-down approach, only suitable for stable environments and first order change and for not, at least overtly, considering organizational politics and power. Burnes (2004), however, reappraises Lewin's concept and challenges the assumptive criticism that it is a simplistic three-stage approach. Burnes highlights that Lewin viewed change as non-linear and as unpredictable—self-interest that manifests itself through politicised conformance adds to non-linearity and unpredictability, and challenges the degree of managerial control outside of hierarchical line management. The problem, however, is not one of identifying resistance, but the degree to which individuals are resisting in an overt politicised way: outwardly espousing their understanding for the need to change, but inwardly not accepting, or fully accepting, the change due to the disruption it causes to individuals, for example, seemingly inconsequential issues such as desk space.

However, this does not mean that individuals do not understand an organization's rationale for change, or even do not understand how change relates to organizational goals. The issue is one to do with personal loss of those aspects of an individual's work routine and networks within formal organizational spaces that are not only valued by individuals, but also enable work to be undertaken efficiently and effectively, even in terms of work that takes place within liminal spaces within organizations. Placing individuals at the centre of change in a political sense raises the issue of the degree of control organizations have through planned change. There is, of course, control, through politicised conformance—more on this later—but not to the extent to which managers think, or perhaps, choose to think. Choosing to assume there is control through planned change predicated on hierarchical power is a safer and easier place to reside as part of organizational dominant space—it is a form of managerial oikeiosis. Oikeiosis will be discussed later in the chapter.

Specifically, in relation to managing change, to what extent, irrespective of the change approach used, do managers—the ones invariably tasked with managing change once the initial flurry of activity is complete—understand this particular force at play, but also the extent to which it cannot be totally controlled through being managerial? Further to this, and in terms of politics as games, Mintzberg, Ahlstrand and Lampel (1998, p234) use a passage from George Elliot's (Mary Anne Evans–George Eliot, 1866) *Felix Holt, The Radical*, which encapsulates the power dynamic between land owners and other stakeholders in relation to 1832 Reform Act. The line, "Fancy what a game of chess would be if all the chessmen had passions and intellects", captures the very essence of the analogy, which is not as esoteric as one may think at first sight in relation to managing organizational change. It relates to change, control, power, resistance and reaction between stakeholding groups, some of whom have more to lose and/or gain than others, and has a self-interest perspective. Simply replace the Reform Act with that of organizational change, and stakeholders with employees, and the analogy fits both organizational life and organizational change. Managers, on behalf of organizations, expect employees to behave as if chess pieces: to conform to the movements dictated through a change process, and to do so irrespective of the approach used. Unfortunately, the chess pieces in the game of change do think for themselves and view the impact of proposed changes in relation to impact on self. Maintenance and control of individual independence of thought, and to a degree action, is through the inner-self; but employees also know that performance through conformance is expected. This presents individuals with a conundrum, that is, to perform through participating in change that requires degrees of conformance, or to set oneself openly against the change, which usually carries a political cost. The result of this is a kind of game playing, but a game where both sides retain forms of control whilst at the same time lacking total control, which adds to the complexity of managing change. A question arises from this, who controls change and the nature of change processes used? The game has rules of politicised conformance behaviour; however, the rules are unwritten, unpublishable and rarely openly spoken of through the formal side of organization, but it is power that managers know exists and enables them to manage. Individuals know the unspoken rules, and are used for shaping thought and action with others within liminal spaces through into formal dominant spaces. This creates a power dynamic that shapes the degree of change through individuals, both in terms of the depth of individual change, and in a temporal sense.

Individuals learn and develop self-interest politicised behaviour; it is experiential, reflexive and reflective in nature; a form of psychological ontogeny, that is, the way individuals develop from a young age into and through adulthood, including work. Learning political behaviour, generally, and at work, enables individuals to achieve a form of oikeiosis, which relates to making oneself at home in one's surroundings; and in the politicised behaviour sense, generally, and at work, feeling at ease through fitting-in. In the work-based context, understanding organizational politics enables individuals to make a conscious link between political activity and job performance (Hochwarter, Witt and Kacmar, 2000) as a means of achieving oikeneiosis. In a more specific sense, oikeiosis can mean appropriation, orientation, familiarisation, affinity, affiliation and endearment. This more specific interpretation of the word lends itself to the way in which individuals behave in relation to the choices they make; again, either in the general social and familial context and/or at work. The process, which all individuals go through, becomes oikeiotes—a sense of belonging through understanding political dynamics of organizational culture. Belonging may seem a strange word to use as it implies embracing the political dynamic in an active and positive sense; however, the word is symbolic, in that it encapsulates the degree of political decision-making that all employees have to do in order to belong, to be able to work within an organization and with colleagues, and to be accepted. Individuals work out the rules of the game through an organization's informal culture, irrespective of any narrative that may exist through an organization's formal culture, which leads to a fluid symbiotic relationship between the formal and informal side of organizations. Such fluidity, of course, will shape specific political decision-making on the part of individuals, which further complicates managing change beyond control exerted through the formal side of organization.

Another aspect of oikeiosis is that it can be related to conscious decisions about political behaviour at work guided by self-interest; and by doing so, allows a more nuanced understanding of the way in which individual political thought and behaviour enables active and/or passive "political ease" at work, whether within formal or informal organizational spaces. The process and action of politicised ease has centrality to individual perception of, and response to, organizational change and how it guides individual thoughts and actions in a political sense, namely:

- Familiarisation—understanding the political dynamic within context: political norms, expectations, acceptable, allowable, locus exercising of power.
- Affinity—personal feelings towards political dynamic and how it fits with one's ethos, which requires individuals to make a politicised decision to "play the game or not" and how this translates into taking decisions with regard to one's political behaviour.
- Appropriation—recognising and taking on political cultural norms, or those aspects that individuals choose to accept in relation to individual ethos, which can manifest itself in a passive or active sense through actions and words.
- Endearment—a decision to more fully embrace the political dynamic in an active sense; or conversely, to reject the political dynamic, which may range from antipathy through estranged to alienation.
- Orientation—positioning oneself in order to fit-in, achieve one's agendum and/or to get things done.

Part of fitting-in politically requires individuals to be either passive or active with regard to politicised behaviour: to do (behaviour) and say certain things (a form of script), or not to do and say certain things in relation to an individual's familiarisation through to the orientation phase. An individual's decision-making process in determining their political response, and therefore their orientation, becomes conscious in order to become at ease within context. Ease in this sense does not however mean that individuals are at ease with proposed changes. It means that individuals are at ease within themselves and with others as to what they really think relative to visible actions and words; it is a settlement owned and controlled by individuals beyond managerial control, and a form of control reflected through degrees of participation in change.

Another aspect of political orientation is the degree to which individuals may seek a form of political capital through formal and informal networks, hierarchies and attendant positional power bases, power bases revolving around individuals (personal power) and connective power. Individuals make a conscious decision to be political in an active and/or passive sense. This is not to say that behaviour is fixed; individual political behaviour may be dependent on the relative importance of contextualised issues. Using political capital as power to benefit self and/or others in an enlightened self-interest way, and in terms of change, may be more to do with maintaining that already held: maintaining self through eroding belief in proposed changes in order to maintain position, role, influence, social networks, promotion prospects etc. Individuals may resist in a *sotto voce* closed sense, that is, politicised action and/or reaction to change that is demonstrated in such a way as to confirm participation, albeit in a closed conformance sense. Individuals will openly discuss their true beliefs and feelings on proposed changes with trusted colleagues; however, such conversations, of course, will tend to remain unknown to managers. This creates, as stated earlier, a power dynamic that is impossible to shape by managers because control of it resides within individuals; control that is known by individuals and used to shape managers to a greater degree than is hitherto recognised. To recognise it, is admission that control does not entirely reside within and through hierarchy, even though proskyneis is practised, and therein lies the duality of control and power between organization and individuals based on self-interest.

Individuals at work also learn through stories, memes, interpretation, discourse, transmission chains, active constructors, actors and actants. Individuals therefore learn how to do politics, whether actively or passively. This process also identifies political behaviour and attendant consequences, whether functional or dysfunctional. Individuals undertake a conceptual analysis of logical implications of behaving in a political way in terms of preferences, choices and means–end schemes; individuals behave in a praxeological way. The role of individuals in proskynesis does, as identified by Hierocles, place individuals at the centre (McGuire and Hutchings, 2006), and, outside of the political forces at play within organizations, an individual's inner-self cannot be managed (Hesson and Olpin, 2013), except, of course, by the individual. Politicised conformance based on self-interest as part of organizational change becomes one of gains and losses that are not optimal, but allow individuals to make and take decisions that, overall, benefit the individual—a form of return on investment in a homo economicus sense. Politicised behaviour is inherent within individual decision-making, and done so, arguably, in relation to Prospect Theory (Kahneman and Tversky, 1979): the choice between pro-balistic alternatives that involve risk, with decisions based on losses and gains rather than outcomes; real life choices rather than optimal decisions. Decision-making based on self-interest is, as put forward by Luke (1974) based on three dimensions of behaviour:

- One-Dimensional behaviour—subjective interests
- Two Dimensional—observable conflict, current and potential issues
- Three Dimensional—political decision-making and control over the agenda.

The three dimensions, I suggest, can be related to the degree to which self-interest is embedded within the act of proskynesis; again, it is something that individuals consciously decide to do, either in an emotive or rationale way. This creates a rational-emotional paradox (Sheard, Kakabadse and Kakabadse, 2011), in that, individuals' attempt to balance rationality and emotionality, and how best to modify behaviour(s) to achieve a balanced relationship between involvement/non-involvement, and emotional engagement and emotional disengagement in relational to the political dynamics of change.

Machiavelli's view on "innovation" (Machiavelli, Skinner and Price, 1988) as change recognises the role that self-interest plays in how individuals make sense of change (sensemaking in relation to organizational sensegiving) and how individuals decide to react. Machiavelli provides a binary response, which is either "enmity" or "luke-warm support", neither of which, if taken literally, is exactly encouraging for the practise of managing change. This implies that even dialogical approaches to managing change will meet with tepidity! Machiavelli is, in one sense, stating the obvious by recognising basic human characteristics through highlighting self-interest in relation to what is lost to and/or gained through change by individuals, and how this will shape resistance: he goes on to refer to those that demonstrate enmity will do so through becoming "partisans" and will fight innovation (change).

This aspect of human nature is a powerful force that shapes how change is internalised, and needs to be not only acknowledged but also discussed to a much greater degree before change commences, during change phases and after change has taken place, especially if there is a desire to manage change from more humanistic perspectives. To understand this does not necessarily mean that it makes managing change easier; in fact, it makes it far more difficult as it raises some uncomfortable truths about work, relationships, power, control, individual and organizational objectives, motivation, and so the list could go on; all of which are not just pertinent to managing change. Machiavelli refers to the concept of truth in terms of effectual as opposed to an imagined ideal—*verita effecttuale* (*The Prince* Ch. 15)—, which emphasises the truthfulness of events in relation to one's actions. Therefore, the truth of change is relative to not only actions taken by organizations, but also individual actions and how they affect outcome pertaining to individual goals.

Change will invariably involve multiple truths at different times, points in a change process: multiple truths, again, driven by individual experience in relation to an espoused organizational truth (story). This aspect of change dynamics will create flux and tension within and between individuals, groups and organizations, which then disrupts the harmony that organizations seek, generally and in relation to change. Organizations want peaceful and stable internal environments as part of holding environment, and do so for the obvious reason of organizational effectiveness. The desire for, at least outwardly, a pacific calm does not represent reality within organizations, beneath the imagined ideal of calmness through harmony there is a natural state of political flux and therefore competing truths; each having its own pull and repulsion. Co-existence of truths, of themselves, does not pull organizations apart; a harmony in one sense exists, but why? The answer may lie in the power extant within and through hierarchy that, politically, employees recognise and conform to; employees know where overt power resides, and their outward political reality is to conform, which maintains harmony, albeit, superficially. It also fits with oikeiosis. However, from an organizational perspective it is a power that, although not spoken about, is used, not in a managed sense, but through knowing the political reality of power through politicised behaviour exhibited within hierarchies.

Does this mean that individuals do not have free choice? The answer to the question is, "yes", in that individuals make choices about conformance in relation to their psychological contract; the balance they decide to have between conformance and non-conformance; to engage or not engage with change; to accept or reject organizational sensegiving; and so on. Individuals, therefore, do have freedom to choose, but choice is very much constrained through hierarchy and attendant formal power bases: individual choice being voiced "openly" through an individual's inner voice, but its manifestation may take a different form from thought. Therefore, managers only hear a politicised voice and behaviour. This, in turn, shapes managerial voice and behaviour, one that usually reflects that change is happening to the degree required; it is, in one sense, rational assumption to make and also allows managers to be at ease—harmony is maintained.

The power imbalance within organizations is part of organizational reality recognised by organizations and employees; it is an accepted fait accompli. Politics, as espoused by Levin (2014, p83) refers to Edmund Burke's (1729–1797) view on politics as juxtaposition to Thomas Paine's (1731–1809) utopian view that politics is not about equality, but one of social peace, prosperity and stability that is important for everyone. Social peace is equally applicable to organization, in that, without harmony through social peace there will be less efficiency, lack of effectiveness and therefore reduced prosperity—continuance of employment, for example. Employees recognise the realpolitik of organizational life and subjugate themselves (proskynesis) accordingly; however, this does not mean complete compliance, but a level of compliance that enables them to signal their commitment to organizational goals. This applies equally to change: Is change based on truth and a true acceptance of what change requires, or is it more to do with levels of politicised conformance in relation to realpolitik? Organizations require a form of political obedience in order to function; employees understand and accept this, just as individuals do in a societal sense, otherwise chaos would reign: ochlocracy (government by the populace); mob rule would take hold and "prosperity" would diminish, and therefore opportunities for self-advancement through change. Individuals do not want this as it is not in individuals' interests; and there being a natural inclination towards structure, order, role etc., in order to get things done. A form of predisposition to towards Weber, Taylor, Fayol, Urwick et al. in recognition of the importance of structure to individuals. This may come across as negative and cynical, and making organizations out to be almost tyrannical and all employees as self-serving, but it is not the intention to do so. It is, through a more nuanced and open exploration of organizational realpolitik, a deeper understanding of how political flux actually shapes attitude and behaviour in relation to change and the efficacy of change methodology. It also fundamentally challenges what actually drives change. Is it, for example, the absolute efficacy of dialogical approaches? Alternatively, is it more to do with politicised conformance; is it, in effect, a dance of realpolitik that brings about a form of comfortable mutual delusion that suits mangers and non-managerial employees?

This aspect of politicised conformance behaviour can be further developed in relation to economic theory, specifically, contract theory whereby an agent conveys information about self to another party in order to create a contract. A contract in a politicised behaviour sense relates to verbal and non-verbal communication of conformance to organizational goals, and in a change sense to the change agenda, in order to avoid a potential cost of non-conformance equitable to economic costs to an individual. Such a contract also allows individuals, if they choose to behave in an active political way, to position themselves through initiating behaviour that is appropriate to the change agendum and/or as a means of avoiding costs associated with non-compliance to expected organizational behavioural norms. Compliance to organizational norms, whether in a goal congruence sense or because of political expediency, maintains "social contract", which, in an anthropological sense (Wright, 1994), maintains a healthy state of equilibrium, at least on the surface. Even so, and from organizational perspective, it maintains order, hierarchy and formal power bases, all of which reinforces a need for individuals to behave in a political way through proskyneis. Such power, as discussed previously, is usually unspoken and rarely seriously challenged; to do so may not be tolerated and possibly carry consequences. Such a power dynamic creates a self-fulfilling loop that is known and understood by employees across all strata, and maintains a delusion of harmonious social contract. Maintenance of a harmonious social contract at work, even allowing for hierarchy, positional power etc., is essential to organizational well-being, efficiency and effectiveness, so to begin to question and discuss individual agenda in a more open way may, for some mangers be very challenging personally. In addition, as Weber (cited in Keyes, 2002) put forward: "man . . . is suspended in webs of significance he himself has spun". Individuals, in relation to how they interpret organizational dynamics in relative to the spinning of such webs (political webs) relate back to familiarisation, affinity, appropriation, endearment, and orientation.

Another way of looking at this is to see politicised conformance as rational political obedience as part of the unspoken, but mutually understood, power relationship contract: individuals as part of the familiarisation phase work out power dynamics in relation to hierarchy, and by conforming in terms of self-interest, even enlightened self-interest, are performing proskynesis. Power within and through hierarchy is a significant shaping force with regard to political behaviour and how individuals see change in relation to their place within organization. This may induce individuals to behave either in a neutral way to change, to go along with it in a passive sense or, based on emotivistic political behaviour, to resist; and, depending on the degree of permissiveness within an organization's prevailing culture, resist openly or through informal network power relationships. If the latter, then this does not preclude individuals performing proskynesis, which will be overt as part of conformance to expected norms. This creates and maintains the duality within individuals' decision-making: conformance and non-conformance will be rational and emotional and shape an individual's political decision-making process.

Individuals are faced with a choice, though not necessarily binary, to focus entirely on self or to try to achieve a balance between self and others and organizational requirements; and doing so in relation to what an individual can live with in terms of personal affinity to participating in organizational politics. Another element within the decision process, and one that cannot be ignored by individuals, relates to organizational citizenship behaviour (OCB), which is a recognition that individuals have to do, to be seen to be doing, certain things in order to demonstrate commitment to organizational goals: individual demonstration of congruency with organizational goal (Witt, 1998). Demonstrating OCB in relation to goal congruence is in itself a form of political behaviour that requires individuals to have consciously moved from familiarisation through to orientation (Randall et al., 1999). The speed of which will be dependent on individual agenda. Individuals will know that in order to fit-in, they have to conform to overt organizational behaviour norms. What an individual really thinks maybe hidden from organization. This creates and/or reinforces a complicit, and as discussed earlier, a politicised delusion between individuals and organization, a delusion that maintains conformity in relation to OCB and goal congruence, hierarchy and concomitant positional power and sense of control. An individual's use of political capital power to benefit self and/or others, generally and in terms of change, can derive from a desire to hold onto those seen as valuable, for example, maintaining self through eroding belief in proposed changes in order to maintain/embody history of our own making, position, role, influence, social networks, promotion prospects etc. Therefore, individuals will resist either openly or in a sotto voce closed sense in relation to self. To reiterate a point made earlier, true political reaction and action to change is, within and through formal organizational settings, hidden, but put into effect through informal settings.

At work, individuals may seek a form of political capital through formal and informal networks, hierarchies and attendant positional power bases, and power bases revolving around individuals (personal power) and, more importantly, connective power. Individuals make a conscious decision, and to use animal typology, become an owl, fox, donkey or sheep (Baddley and James, 1987). This is not to say that behaviour is fixed, it will be dependent on the context and the relative importance of the issue that shapes political decisions made. For example, how individuals perceive change, in terms of gains and losses, as mentioned previously, will determine an internalised response, which may or may not be manifest outwardly. Part of an individual's decision to express their feelings openly and honestly towards proposed changes will be guided by the degree of permissiveness prevalent through the prevailing culture. If the prevailing formal culture is one that is not open and permissive of meaningful constructive dissent then employees will work this out as part of their sensemaking of the political dynamic. Such sensemaking of the degree of unspoken politicised conformance—the degree of proskynesis—sets the tone and the extent of employee participation in dialogue and general interaction, irrespective of exhortations by line managers and/or those tasked with managing change to "tell me/us what you really think".

In conclusion, management, at all levels, is key to setting the tone, creating organizational climate and creating a new way of interaction that reduces the dysfunctional non- proskynesis aspects of organizational political dynamic. This is key to trying to ensure that organizational holding environments minimise the general political aspects in order to provide a safe space for individuals to participate more fully through debate, challenge and, dare one say it, functional conflict. Which is not to say that political behaviour will not be evident on the part of individuals, but, at the very least, the aim should, based on understanding political power and where it resides, be a more sophisticated approach to managing through the political dynamic inherent within organizational change. A form of sophistication that, in order to create "good constitutions", includes a more open approach to discussing politics. What we learn, a politicised sense, through socialisation and acculturation within organizations reduces the propensity for openness, honesty, meaningful debate etc., and gets in the way of creating an effective and self-sustaining learning based organizational culture that could be change oriented in a more meaningful way through reduced politicised conformance. Linked to this is Managerial Narrative (Boje, 2012) and the way in which narrative carries a political dimension. The power of prevailing and past narratives to shape current and future perspectives is an inevitable element within organizational holding environments, thus shaping behaviour in a politicised way. Narratives that are highly politicised get in the way of optimising learning and development as part of change. There is also a tendency to do this in a retrospective sensemaking way (Weick, 1995), in that the past shapes the current that shapes the future, a double loop element wherein retrospective politicised narratives have strong resonance and shape current and future sensemaking which maintains the unspoken settlement.

References

Baddley, S. and James, K. (1987) Owl, Fox, Donkey or Sheep: Political Skills for Managers. *Management Education and Development*, 18(1), 3–19.

Balogun, J. and Hope Hailey, V. (2004) *Exploring Strageic Change* (2nd ed.). Harlow: Financial Times/Prentice Hall.

Beckhard, R. and Harris, R. T. (1987) *Organizational Transitions: Managing Complex Change*, (2nd ed.). Hoboken: Pearson Education.

Boje, D. (2012) Reflections: What Does Quantum Physics of Storytelling Mean for Change Management? *Journal of Change Management*, 12(3), 253–271.

Bolman, L. G. and Deal, T. (1997) *Reframing Organizations: Artistry, Choice, and Leadership* (2nd ed.). San Francisco: Jossey-Bass.

Burnes, B. (2004) Kurt Lewin and the Planned Approach to Change: A Re-Appraisal. *Journal of Management Studies*, 41(6), 913–1056.

Cyert, R. M. and March, J. G. (1963) *A Behavioural Theory of the Firm*. London: Prentice-Hall.

Eliot, G. (1866) *Felix Holt, the Radical*.

Hesson, M. and Olpin, M. (2013) *Stress Management for Life: A Research Based Experiential Approach* (3rd ed.). Andover: Cengage Learning.

Hochwarter, W. A., Witt, L. A. and Kacmar, K. M. (2000) Perceptions of Organizational Politics as a Moderator of the Relationship Between Consciousness and Job Performance. *Journal of Applied Psychology*, 85(3), 472–478.

Kahneman, D. and Tversky, A. (1979) Prospect Theory: An Analysis of Decision Under Risk. *Econometrica*, 47(2), 263.

Keyes, C. F. (2002) Weber and Anthropology. *Annual Review of Anthropology*, 31, 233–255.

Levin, Y. (2014) *The Great Debate Edmund Burke, Thomas Paine and the Birth of Right and Left*. New York: Basic Books.

Lewin, K. (1951) *Field Theory in Social Science*. New York: Harper & Row.

Lukes, S. (1974) *Power: A Radical View*. New York: Macmillan Press.

Machiavelli, N., Skinner, Q. (ed.), and Price, R. (ed.) (1988) *Machiavelli: The Prince*. Cambridge: Cambridge University Press.

McGuire, D. and Hutchings, K. (2006) A Machiavellian Analysis of Organizational Change. *Journal of Organizational Change Management*, 19(2), 192–209

Mintzberg, H., Ahlstrand, B. and Lampel, J. (1998) *Strategy Safari*. London: Prentice Hall.

O'Neill, J. (2001) Self-interest. In *Routledge Encyclopedia of Philosophy*. Taylor and Francis.

Randall, M. I., Cropanzano, R., Borman, C. A. and Burjulin, A. (1999) Organizational Politics and Organizational Support as Predictors of Work Attitudes, Job Performance, and Organizational Citizenship Behaviour. *Journal of Organizational Behaviour*, 20, 159–174.

Routledge Encyclopedia of Philosophy, (1998), New York: Routledge.

Sheard, G., Kakabadse, A. P. and Kakabadse, N. K. (2011) Organizational Politics: Reconciling Leadership's Rational-Emotional Paradox. *Leadership and Organizational, Development Journal*, 32(1), 78–97.

Weick, K. E. (1995) *Sensemaking in Organizations*. London: Sage.

Witt, L. A. (1998) Enhancing Organizational Goal Congruence: A Solution to Organizational Politics. *Journal of Applied Psychology*, 83(40), 666–674.

Wright, S. (1994) *The Anthropology of Organizations*. London: Routledge.

2   Political Narratives of Change

Organizations are not all seeing and powerful—not panoptical—and therefore do not have absolute control over employees' stories and narratives—employees "own" what is within their narrative as part of their stories. Individuals decide what to give, generally, and in relation to change; however, politicised conformance is a reality that we observe and act upon because of and through narrative within stories of change. Individuals reorient their psychological contracts to try to ensure they maintain what they can and/or in relation to what they can gain, and do so, or part of, in relation to their and others' narratives. This runs counter to the general story and narrative of change always being for the betterment of organizations; the assumption tends to be one of maximising through change.

This chapter discusses narratives of change from organizational and individual perspectives, narratives that may hold countervailing views, which, either are, or become, politicised in terms of behaviour. As Buchanan and Dawson (2007) put forward, organizations "fail to accommodate polyvocal narratives of change". Polyphony as part of organizational life is well-researched and understood (Belova, King and Sliwa, 2008), and is an important aspect of understanding managing change in a more nuanced way, especially in relation to multiple-narratives through and across organizational boundaries. Narratives are powerful in shaping what individuals think, both in terms of reinforcing current beliefs and in shaping emerging views (Mumby, 1993). Behaviour, through narrative, that becomes part of the dance of mutual delusion (Bénabou, 2009), which maintains structure, order, role etc., from both organizational and employee perspectives. The word "delusion" is used because the political dynamic, as discussed in Chapter 1, is largely unspoken, yet it is known, so lack of open discussion of the political aspects of change creates a form of settlement that is superficial: organizational change stories are superficial, but individuals' narratives are, from their perspective, deeper and have more meaning. Therefore, the surface calm maintains the "social contract", but it is delusory; however, underneath the surface there will be undercurrents of unvoiced dissention, given voice through informal networks to create a counter-narrative to that of formal organizational narratives. For the purpose of this chapter a slightly abridged version of Toolan's (2001, p8) definition is used: "A narrative is a perceived sequence of non-randomly connected events, typically involving, as the experiencing agonist, humans . . . from whose experience we humans can 'learn'." Individuals, therefore, learn politics of context and its practise through narrative.

Part of the appeal of narrative is that humans enjoy a good story, especially one that fulfils the expected structure of storytelling; we look for key points along the narrative journey, from an understood beginning through to an expected outcome (climax). Organizational politics as part of organizational change provides, through liminal spaces, opportunities for politics to thrive (Sturdy, Schwarz and Spicer, 2006), and a space within which political narratives can emerge, be reinforced and diffused through and across organizational boundaries. The more powerful shaping narratives are those told by actors that have capacity and power to use narrative within storytelling to shape others. Of course, such actors reside within management structures; however, the issue is the extent to which narrative through formal management structures is more powerful in shaping belief when compared to informal network. In addition, how to tell if the formal is more powerful than the informal, or vice-versa, that is, what is actually going on below the surface with regard to political though shaping conformance to the formal narrative? Alongside this, formal and informal networks will provide the structure through which narrative is used, word-of-mouth as the most effective, especially by key actors. The impact of technology, given its widespread use and speed in diffusing story and narrative, will also play its part, what Ferguson, Groenewegen, Moser, Mohr and Borgatti (2017) refer to as offline and online domain relationships within organizations. Relationships that will have as much resonance these days as "water cooler conversations"; and adding another dimension to the dynamic: a dimension that goes beyond organizational boundaries, both internal and external.

Understanding narrative and storytelling are important shaping forces within organizations. Boje (2008, p2) states that, "in storytelling organizations, narrative-control and story diffusion are the force and counter-force of self-organising . . . each organization achieves a unique balance between narrative order and story disorder"; he also makes the point that narrative has become a "centring force of control and order". The view that storytelling and narrative both play an important part in organizational life also relates to their role within organizational change (Boje, 1991), in that change does not take place within a vacuum, but takes place within extant structures and culture, so narrative and stories will co-exist and evolve. Given this, those individuals that shape narratives within and through change, may be able to shape the dynamic, though not control it. Shaping narrative, whether through formal and/or informal means, is a form of power that plays a key part in creating a desire to change and in embedding change.

In Chapter 1, I referred to the change equation (Balogun and Hope Hailey, 2004), and it is worth briefly revisiting it at this point, specifically, the role that narratives and their politicised content play within the equation, even though narrative and politics are not specifically mentioned. Narrative is, however, an undercurrent that plays a part in shaping each of the phases of the equation, as is the case within all change frameworks. For example, if satisfaction and/or dissatisfaction relationship is considered, then if desirability of proposed changes is low, a narrative will be created to support the continuance of the current; a narrative that may or may not be shared openly depending on prevailing organizational political climate set through hierarchy and managerial action. If individuals do not communicate their individual narrative, or replicate that of a generally held narrative, in a transparent way then it will take on a more political dimension through closed behaviour and language that is used as part of dialogue: not sharing the story or couching language and terms used through formal communication mechanisms used within the change process.

The remaining elements of the equation, namely, practicality and cost, will create, depending on what the change represents, a politicised narrative through behaviour, the open/closed aspects. Like most other change frameworks, the equation does not mention political narrative in any explicit sense; however, they should do so, though not as a means of quantifying it, but to recognise that it is inherent within change (Boyce, 1996) and not ignored in terms of its power to shape individual beliefs and actions, and to do so through narrative. At the very least, politicised narrative shaping politicised behaviour needs to become far more prominent than it otherwise is, and no longer be an unmentionable part of organizational life that everyone knows and understands, but feels unable to discuss openly and honestly in terms of the role that self-interest plays and how it shapes behaviour.

Employees have power through using narrative, more so than organizations assume and/or admit; politicised narrative power being used in such a way as to go beyond a general understanding of what motivates individuals in a content and/or process sense. Organizations tend to gravitate to a narrative of change that is usually linear and temporal in orientation, a narrative to which employees adhere through politicised conformance. One perspective is to see employees controlling narratives, ones that they regard as "true", especially in relation to their reality of self and their place within organizational change. Employee perception in terms of "true" narrative will determine how they see meaning and impact of proposed changes, and how to conform to the requirements of change relative to what they wish to try to hold on to, and what they wish to "give" in a satisficing sense. Irrespective of what an organization communicates as part of its narrative of change, individuals will create their own narrative within their story of change (past, present and future) that is their version of reality (Berger and Luckmann, 1967). Individual versions of reality—individual truth—therefore comes from a constructivist perspective, each individual narrative is a subjective interpretation of reality (Thier, 2018, p15), a reality which individuals own and control.

Another element to be considered is representation of image as part of politicised conformance behaviour, specifically, action on the part of individuals that conform to expectations; expectations that are part of the formal and informal aspects of organizational life. Individual actions in relation to what a change agenda requires may be entirely genuine and representative of an individual's commitment; and used to signal commitment, this based on the view that actions do not lie. However, such a simple acceptance of an individual's commitment to change does not take account of the duality that exists between action and belief, to use Frankish's (2009) terminology, "partial and flat-out belief". The degree to which an individual's attitude determines belief or partial belief will shape an individual's acceptance of not only the rationale for change, but also the extent to which the change will, in a change equation sense, affect self.

Ownership of politicised narrative power is, in a general organizational sense, accepted, but rarely openly acknowledged and discussed. Such a settlement as part of organizational social contract (Keeley, 1988) may enable organizations to rely, in a passive sense, on politicised conformance to bring about change even though the existence of countervailing narratives may exist. Managers leave this aspect of change unsaid and in place; and therein lies a paradox concerning the means by which organizations manage change, whether linear or non-linear in orientation. Perversely, a politicised satisficing (Mohr, 1994) response to change may fit organizational narratives of change. Mutually assured delusion, mentioned earlier, may suit both managerial and non-managerial employees, in that it creates a settlement based on an acceptance of the status quo that neither side wishes to challenge openly, a force that shapes and maintains mutually unspoken/unshared change narratives.

Breaking the inherent politicised conformance within narratives resides with employees, irrespective of management's desire to create dialogue. Managers may try to set a dialogical tone, but employees decide on the degree to which they participate, so "own" it as a form of politicised power. If this is the case, it is in an organization's self-interest to rely on and pursue formal narratives in order to: (1) reinforce the change message,

(2) to maintain the change plan, (3) to reinforce adherence to the change approach used, (4) to reinforce the outcome stage—it has worked / was successful. At one level, this is understandable as change is complex (Greenwood, Raynard, Kodeih, Micelotta and Lounsbury, 2017) and has its own non-linearity, irrespective of an obvious desire on the part of managers to provide clear direction through planned and structured linearity, even as part of dialogical approaches to managing change. Organizational milieu is, at the best of times, an amorphous mass moving in a co-ordinated direction confined by holding environment, yet is constrained and unconstrained at the same time: the tension between formal and informal organizational culture in relation to individual agency. In addition, and as Jarrett (2008) argues within his "seven myths", managers cannot manage change; the point being, managers are not in control of all aspects as change, through employees' hidden political agenda, it creates a political life, with accompanying narrative, of its own. Once a process of change is underway, managers begin to lose degrees of control over the process. However, organizations, through hierarchy and delineated managerial positional power, maintain and sustain direction of change primarily through formal control.

Employees' self-interest will bring about politicised conformance, thus conforming to organizational expectations, but do so without relinquishing control. This is not, however, to justify non-action in relation to trying to understand another dimension of change. Understanding the relationship between narrative and organizational dynamics (Geiger and Antonacopoulou, 2009) may, through setting a more non-politicised tone, enable those tasked with managing change to have more open and honest dialogue as part of change. Inculcating a more open and honest dialogue in order to try and gain a more nuanced understanding of politicised self-interest will not necessarily remove politicised conformance shaped by narrative, or bring about a greater degree of control. It should, however, be seen as a developmental process before, during and after change; one that begins to engender more meaningful discussions to understand individual perception and narrative, and likely reaction to change, and may, through tapping into an organization's informal dimension, bring wider benefits to organizational performance (Gulati and Puranam, 2009).

Some individuals will be passive within the narrative process, that is, they act as a conduit for the dissemination of narratives through their networks, which also, in one sense, allows them to become part of the narrative within the change story. From this, such individuals may become more active as part of the diffusion process, to become more involved in the story: to support or create resistance to the change. Narrative, including being part of it, can therefore embolden individuals to participate; it may also persuade individuals not to participate, again, this will be dependent on individual agenda and how they fit their narrative: political self-interest will be the dominating deciding factor. Other individuals will have a clear political agenda, and will create, develop, and even embellish, narrative in order to influence others. Those individuals who have a strong influential personal power base may use it maximise the impact of their narrative, or to reinforce a collective narrative in relation to individual and/or shared agenda. This does not exclude the use of positional power based networks for narrative diffusion, and as a means of building alliances in order to effect and/or affect agenda (Buchanan and Badham, 2008). Formal and informal networks are, of course, not mutually exclusive, but will very much overlap and increase the rate and extent of diffusion, adding to the way in which narratives evolve in an organic way, though key elements will be maintained (Polkinghorne, 1988): those elements provide consistency of narrative, especially if they chime with a collective interpretation of change. In addition, those individuals with a strong political agendum, and who have strong personal and/or positional power, will wish to retain and reinforce those elements of narrative that suit their views, to reinforce what is situated within them.

In order to explore further the role of narrative within change and how narratives become politicised, narrative can be broken down into distinct elements; elements that individuals expect, look for and use in order to frame their own understanding and for transmission to others. Narrative is a conscious structured process that enables its creators and recipients to make sense of story in context, both in an internal and external monologue sense (Díaz, 2013). Externalised political narrative on the part of employees will be within trusted network, but with a different story narrative aired through formal spaces. This reinforces the duality of the way in which narrative becomes manifest through individuals and as part of informal community stories. Managers tasked with managing change will not know what an individual's internal narrative is, unless, of course, an individual communicates it through an effective dialogical approach based on deeper levels of trust and reciprocal respect between management and non-managerial employees. Any externalised narrative through trusted networks will also remain unknown, or at best part known, by management, and reinforces the complexity of managing change and the degree of control that organizations have over narrative once an organization communicates the "official" change story. Employees will shape their narrative in relation to an organization's change story, which creates multiple interpretations and iterations; the story takes on a life of its own and is therefore beyond the control of management. However, the issue at this point, is the extent to which the power of politicised narrative through informal spaces is more powerful than an organization's script for change manifest through controlling change through hierarchy and line management.

In the broad sense, narrative, in order to attract listeners and therefore shape their senesmaking, will typically have a plot that is about to happen or is unfolding through events: characters, both major and minor roles (actors and actants); conflict in the form of obstacles, problems or things to be overcome/resolved; and themes/key messages. All these are relatable to organization per se, and specifically in relation to organizational change as follows:

1. *The plot*—proposed changes and implications, broad and specific to self. The plot as organizational agenda, story and narrative; and, conversely, individual agenda, story and narrative.
2. *Characters*—senior management, line management, non-managerial employees; some of whom of course either will take on specific roles (actors) through position within hierarchy, or roles ascribed by others. Ascribed roles that are positive—providing power to shape narrative and others that goes well beyond the shaping power of positional roles and concomitant narratives. In addition, an ascribed role will be the story teller(s) who, if operating from a strong personal power base, can become the "pied piper" of the narrative.
3. *Conflict*—organizational expectations of change and employee performance in relation to individual interpretation of proposed changes and impact on self, which raises the questions: What to do? To whom should one listen? Which narrative to follow? And so on.
4. *Themes/key message*—what is the narrative saying in a broad and specific sense, and can the key message(s) be easily understood, whether through the use of direct language and/or through metaphor.

Underpinning the broad structure of narrative there are specific elements that also need to be present in the form of typical characteristics, namely: (1) construction, (2) prefabrication, (3) trajectory, (4) preliminary orientations, (5) the speaker/teller, (6) displacement, (7) reference points and recalling events. Each element of the structure needs to be in place to fulfil individual and collective expectations of story and storyline; any element that is missing will dilute the impact of both narrative and the story: we begin to stop listening, irrespective of who generates the story, whether senior management or by storytellers within informal networks.

1. *Construction*
   Organizational stories of change will have a structure that will aim to set out the rationale for change, and do so through using the usual language associated with change, within which will be a narrative of expected co-operation, participation and acceptance of proposed

changes. The story and narrative of change created by management, usually constructed without meaningful discourse analysis (Tsoukas, 2005), is done in order to make the change message more meaningful and, ideally, accepted to a greater degree, and therefore minimising counter-narratives being created by employees. The operative word at this point is very much "attempting", as once released, the story will, as discussed previously, have an uncontrolled life of its own, and control will pass from management to employees. However, discourse analysis will be used to a greater degree by employees within informal spaces, which will shape and reinforce employees' identification with proposed changes in relation to self.

The degree to which individuals identify with proposed changes requires individuals to make a political decision on conformance behaviour; behaviour that demonstrates the required organizational citizen behaviour characteristics (Van Dick et al., 2006) in order to demonstrate identification with, and conformance to, change agenda. Those employees that have known power to shape others through informal networks will carefully select language, sequence of the narrative, its emphasis and even pace; such individuals may also rehearse narrative in order to develop its effectiveness. Depending on the strength of their power base, such individuals, in relation to the degree to which other employees meaningfully identify (not politicised conformance) with an organization's values and norms, will be able to shape the change dynamic. At the very least, they may attempt to shape the dynamic as best they can; they become agents of change in relation to their agenda!

2. *Prefabrication*
    This relates to those parts of a narrative that employees have heard before, or employees think they have heard, therefore, individuals, depending on the narrative, may be predisposed to its acceptance (Ding, 2018). Predisposition will relate to organizational narrative as well as narratives created through informal networks, and will elicit a response based on analysis and interpretation to guide behaviour. Prefabrication provides individuals with cues from which to reinforce their schematic beliefs, their interpretation of context in relation to self and how it translates into action. This, as part of narrative, enables those that wish to try and shape the change dynamic to use words and phrases that will meet prefabricated elements: the trigger words that will illicit an expected response. Organizations do the same, use words to emphasise, in a refabricated sense, that, for example, change is a necessity, is urgent and will take on a form relevant to organizational needs. Interpretation of prefabricated words rests, of course, with individuals, they

control what they think in relation to conformance and the degree of proskynesis they demonstrate.

3. *Trajectory*

Narratives usually have a trajectory, in that, part of their purpose in an organizational change sense, is to have a destination, though not necessarily a formal homecoming. Narrative trajectory in the organizational sense should be seen as a journey that individuals create and maintain in order to make sense of what is happening, to determine action and also to get to a certain place that they feel comfortable with. A place that is both internalised and externalised, a place they wish to be and/or feel comfortable with their decision on the balance they wish to achieve between expected organizational citizen behaviour and politicised conformance behaviour. Organizations maintain direction of travel through continued repeating of the change message and through co-ordination and structure of change. However, the subtext narrative is outside of organizational control, so there will be multiple journey experiences on the part of employees. Journeys, in a duality sense, that will have both a destination as idealised by managers, but also individual destinations that fit the self.

4. *Preliminary Orientations*

This relates to the direction in which individuals expect a narrative to take them, an expected outcome for the story, organizational and individual outcomes with regard to change. Narrative orientation will be different for each individual, and if heard before, it will shape an individual's orientation in relation to previous experience of change. Depending on the strength of an organization's narrative, the direction of an individual's orientation will remain fixed in line with their defined trajectory. This aspect of narrative usually goes undiscussed, therefore the conflicting orientations very rarely come to light: they may be known, but remain unknowable due to lack of discussion based on politicised decisions either by managers not to ask, or for non-managerial employees not wishing to be open about their orientation in relation to agenda based on self-interest.

5. *The Speaker/Teller*

Narratives require someone to tell the narrative and someone, others, to listen and even become part of the narrative in an actor or actant sense. Within change, organizations instigate their stories and narrative through hierarchy in order to address employees through forms of mass communication. Organizations, after the initial phase, will devolve communication of the change message to line managers who therefore become actors within the narrative, in that they become part of the narrative through not just communicating the change message, but also how they interpret and use language. Managers also become actants, in the ascribed sense, in the eyes of non-managerial employees: they perform an expected function within the narrative, the bringer of good or bad news, for example. Through informal networks, individuals will also instigate story and create a narrative, they become the teller of the tale, a tale that some will construct in a politicised sense in order to shape others through the use of language in order to tap into an expected change orientation.

6. *Displacement*

    Narrative uses displacement to refer to events removed from the space and time in which they exist. Change provides many opportunities for the use of displaced references within the creation and maintenance of narrative; displaced events that will be part of the collective memory, that is, events in the experiential sense, old stories and forms of folk memory. The focus here is on displacement having more resonance within and through informal networks, which provides myriad opportunities to tap into potential rich veins of stories and narratives. Those individuals wishing to create, even recreate if relevant, a narrative or counter-narrative, will know which stories and narrative to tap into in order to make, even embellish, old and/or distant events relevant to the current. Moreover, it will be done so in the form of lessons learnt and to be learnt, and therefore to be listened to. Spatially and temporally distant events may be used to exploit those aspects of proposed changes to suit agenda based on interpretation and interpolation of events. Individuals will be selective in their choice to reinforce their orientation to change generally, and in relation to orientation within narrative, which will shape their politicised conformance behaviour.

7. *Reference to/Recalling Events*

    This aspect of narrative focuses on the recall of specific events to reinforce a new narrative; it goes beyond using anecdote. Furthermore, remoteness in a spatial and temporal sense is not a hindrance to creating a narrative. The recall of specific events adds weight to a narrative, to create truth through evidence. Moreover, the more specific events are, the more truthful the evidence and therefore the more influential the narrative, whether in terms of impact on the collective or individual. The more politicised the narrative the more selective the recall, the process becomes highly selective in order to support fit individual schema through stereotyping and bias. Furthermore, the more that recalled events appeal to emotion the more influential they will be: emotion within storytelling is, generally, very influential; and individuals look for emotional attachment through story, and also do so at work (Buskirk and McGrath, 1992). The emotional aspect to a story's appeal may well outweigh rational expectations on the part of organization with regard to the degree to which employees fully accept and commit to what change requires of them through organizational citizen behaviours.

Each element of narrative structure is mutually inclusive; each element needs to be in place in order for narrative to be effective through listeners' expectations of what a good, interesting and useful story should provide. Lack of any of the elements will limit narrative impact and therefore its diffusion, which further reduces its impact throughout an organization. This applies to both organizational and individual levels. However, if narrative is lacking and/or lacks structure it does not mean that individuals will not wish to create one. If narrative is missing, individuals will create their own to fill the void, the extent to which individual narratives will then coalesce at some point into a form of collective narrative will depend on the extant dynamic within holding environments. If narrative resides at the individual level then it becomes more self-centred and self-fulfilling in relation to individual impact.

In conclusion, the decisions that individuals make based on their degree of belief will determine their actions towards change. Within this, individuals will have worked out, relative to their degree of belief, the extent to which conformance through action is required, this being a political decision. Individuals, once they have internalised their political orientation to change, will act in line with organizational expectations of conformance to the requirements of the change, but may do so without altering their true beliefs with regard to the meaning and impact of the change.

A very pertinent proposition at this point is the extent to which organizations have to be concerned with the inner-self beliefs of employees, the main concern being one of employee conformance actions of going along with change. This proposition will, for many, raise particular concerns, in that it challenges, at least to some degree, the validity of using dialogical approaches to managing change based on employee participation. The intention is not, as stated in the introduction to this book, to undermine the validity and efficacy of dialogical approaches to managing change, but to introduce a more realistic consideration of the role that politicised conformance plays in shaping actual behaviour based on individual beliefs shaped by narrative, and how individuals respond in an emotional way to change.

References

Balogun, J. and Hope Hailey, V. (2004) *Exploring Strategic Change*, Harrow: Prentice Hall Financial Times.

Belova, O., King, I. and Sliwa, M. (2008) Introduction: Polyphony and Organization Studies: Mikhail Bakhtin and Beyond. *Organizational Studies*, 29(4), 493–500.

Bénabou, R. (2009) *Groupthink: Collective Delusions in Organizations and Markets*. NBER Working Paper No. 14764. Retrieved January 2012 from Princeton University.

Berger, H. S. and Luckmann, T. (1967) *The Social Construction of Reality*. New York: Anchor.

Boje, D. M. (1991) Consulting and Change in the Storytelling Organization. *Journal of Organizational Change Management*, 4(3) 7–1.

Boje, D. M. (2008) *Storytelling Organizations*. London: Sage.

Boyce, M. E. (1996) Organizational Story and Storytelling: A Critical Review. *Journal of Organizational Change Management*, 9(5), 5–26.

Buchanan, D. A. and Badham, R. J. (2008) *Power, Politics and Organizational Change Winning the Turf Game* (2nd ed.). London: Sage Publications.

Buchanan, D. A. and Dawson, P. (2007) Discourse and Audience: Organizational Change as Multi-Story Process, *Journal of Management Studies*, 44(5), 669–686.

Díaz, J.-L. (2013) A Narrative Method for Consciousness Research. *Frontiers in Human Neuroscience*, 7, 739.

Ding, J. (2018) *Linguistic Prefabrication A Discourse Analysis Approach*. Singapore: Springer.

Ferguson, J. E., Groenewegen, P., Moser, C., Mohr, J. W. and Borgatti, S. P. (eds.) (2017) *Structure, Content and Meaning of Organizational Networks* (Research in the Sociology of Organizations, Volume 53). Bingley, UK: Emerald Publishing Limited, 1–15.

Frankish, K. (2009) Partial Belief and Flat-Out Belief. In F. Huber and C. Schmidt-Petri (eds.), *Degrees of Belief*. Synthese Library (Studies in Epistemology, Logic, Methodology, and Philosophy of Science, Volume 342). Dordrecht: Springer.

Geiger, D. and Antonacopoulou, E. (2009) Narratives and Organizational Dynamics Exploring Blind Spots and Organizational Inertia. *The Journal of Applied Behavioral Science*, 45(3), 411–436.

Greenwood, R., Raynard, M., Kodeih, F., Micelotta, E. R. and Lounsbury, M. (2017) Institutional Complexity and Organizational Responses. *Academy of Management Annals*, 5(1), 317–371.

Gulati, R. and Puranam, P. (2009) Renewal Through Reorganization: The Value of Inconsistencies Between Formal and Informal Organization. *Organization Science*, 20(2), 281–480.

Jarrett, M. (2008) The Seven Myths of Change Management. *Business Strategy Review*, 1(4), 22–29.

Keeley, M. (1988) *A Social-Contract Theory of Organizations*. University of Notre Dame Press.

Mohr, B. L. (1994) Authority in Organizations: On the Reconciliation of Democracy and Expertise. *Journal of Public Administration Research and Theory*, 4(1), 49–66.

Mumby, D. K. (1993) *Narrative and Social Control: Critical Perspectives* (Sage Annual Review of Communications Research). Thousand Oaks, Sage Publications.

Polkinghorne, D. E. (1988) *Narrative Knowing and the Human Science*. Albany: State University of New York.

Sturdy, A., Schwarz, M. and Spicer, A. (2006) Guess Who's Coming to Dinner? Structures and Uses of Liminality in Strategic Management Consultancy. *Human Relations*, 59(7), 929–960.

Thier, K. (2018) Storytelling. In *Organizations: A Narrative Approach to Change, Brand, Project and Knowledge Management*. Berlin Heidelberg: Springer.

Toolan, M. (2001) *Narrative: A Critical Linguistic Introduction* (2nd ed.). London: Routledge.

Tsoukas, H. (2005) Afterword: Why Language Matters in the Analysis of Organizational Change. *Journal of Organizational Change Management*, 18(1), 96–104.

Van Buskirk, W. and McGrath, D. (1992) Organizational Stories as a Window on Affect in Organizations. *Journal of Organizational Change Management*, 5(2), 9–24.

Van Dick, R., Grojean, M. W., Christ, O. and Wieske, J. (2006) Identity and the Extra Mile: Relationships Between Organizational Identification and Organizational Citizenship Behaviour. *British Journal of Management*, 17, 283–301.

3 Illusion of Control

This chapter discusses the degree to which organizations have control over employee political attitudes and behaviour through change. Politicised conformance through politicised behaviour (Schein, 1977), as already discussed in the preceding chapters, is inherent within change and takes on different forms relative to individuals' sensemaking of the perceived impact of change, and does so in relation to an organization's culture (Harris, 1994). Dependent on the nature of proposed changes, individuals will act out of self-interest and reorient their psychological contract in order to maintain their current sense of reality, or reorient their "contract" toward what can be gained through change, even if in an enlightened self-interest way (De Dreu, 2004; De Dreu and Nauta, 2009). Individuals demonstrate their reorientation through behaviour and language, but not in a unified sense, that is, individuals will adopt behaviour and language that signals conformance within formal spaces and adjust both within informal spaces: individuals demonstrating politically divisible behaviour in relation to context. This view, based on a form of anthropological realism (Herzfeld, 2017), runs counter to the general narrative of change through collective employee buy-in based on unitary goals, thus being for the betterment of the whole.

It is part of human nature to think in self-interested terms and therefore part of the reality of society, and organizations. The reality of organizational life is one of political power through employees and in relation to management structures. Individuals cannot escape the political reality and power relationships of organizational life, as it is everywhere, even within liminal spaces: it is an inherent anthropological dimension within organizational psychodynamics. Even if an organization wishes to try to de-politicise interactions—reduce at best—it will not succeed, in that individuals will still think and behave politically irrespective of organizational rhetoric and action. Therefore, the question that arises is, if actions are the words that never lie and should have power to shape the political dynamic, then why do employees still behave in a passive or active way politically? The loci of power and control within organizations is at the heart of the answer to the question, and how individual behaviour, in relation to organizational power bases, shapes responses demonstrated through proskynesis. Proskynesis is a recognition that power, in a structural hierarchical sense, resides upwards, and individuals will reflect this in relation to their general politicised behaviour and relative to their and others' positions within hierarchy (Brass and Burkhardt, 1993).

Language as part of proskynesis through conversation is a powerful means–end to signal intent, whether meant or not, and is used by individuals to shape others' perceptions. Language and conversation become a cloak underneath which individuals cover actual intent, especially within formal organizational spaces. Ford (1999) sees organization as being composed of multi-conversations through networks that create "conversational realities", realities that shape attitude and behaviour and are both key aspects of organizational life generally and in relation organizational change. Added to this, is that conversation is not static; it changes through the inclusion of new and different perspectives as points of contact increase through formal and informal networks. Conversation as a means of diffusing narrative through informal networks is very powerful: words will be more influential, depending on, and in relation to, organizational action and/or inaction and will be used by employees to shape narratives, especially by those individuals that are trusted and therefore have a degree of personal power (Elias, 2008). Individuals that have personal power within and through informal networks are able to become key actors and take on the role of change agent, and depending on how they view proposed changes, become either advocates of detractors of proposed changes. They become nodal points within the social network (Tichy, Tushman and Fombrun, 1979; Borgatti, Mehra, Brass and Labianca, 2009) and can act as a filter and embellishers of narrative through conversation.

Conversation provides a framework through which individuals are able to keep in touch, share experiences and perspectives, spread misinformation and spread rumour and, of course, gossip (Kurland and Hope Pelled, 2000). Individuals also use conversation, either as active or passive participants, to create, maintain and extend relations, or of equal importance, solidarity with like-minded individuals. This aspect of organizational social networks also provides individuals with a means to reconcile their rational-emotional response based on their values and norms relative to proposed changes. Specifically, it provides a means to express explicitly their emotional investment in relation to the importance they place on proposed changes in relation to self-interest. This, within the context of change and politicised conformance, provides individuals with a means by which thought, attitude and action can coalesce around a common interpretation of their sense of meaning and reality of change: it provides belonging, comfort, support and a base from which to resist change in relation to their power to do so.

Conversation within and through organizational grapevines enables effective diffusion of narrative to take place at rates that overtake formal communications. Grapevines as part of informal networks are far more powerful that official channels; it is an aspect of organizational life that is beyond the control of management (Crampton, Hodge and Mishra, 1998) and shapes agenda to a greater degree than organizations may wish to acknowledge, at least not openly acknowledge. Management communicating the rational and nature of proposed changes through structural formal channels (Baker, 2009) will invariably conflict in some way with a change narrative communicated through informal networks, which at the individual level will require decisions to be taken on which narrative to accept and conform to, and to what degree. Individuals will make political conformance decisions based on self-interest relative to not only the perceived impact of proposed changes on them in terms of disruption to routine etc., but also the extent to which explicit demonstration of conformance words and behaviour will be required. The tension between formal organizational change narratives, and narratives that exist within informal spaces, will, as already discussed, shape behaviour. The degree to which narrative shapes attitude and behaviour will be dependent on the strength of the narratives relative to self. Concomitant with this is that individuals will maintain an inner conversation in relation to their real beliefs and thus shape attitude, but outwardly express, in some acceptable form to self and management, conformance behaviour: individuals make and take a politicised decision.

If organizations have a desire to use dialogue to bring about change then words alone will not be enough. To give meaning to words used through formal means of communication, managers must demonstrate action in order for the words to have meaning and impact. Employees see through rhetoric, and base their interpretation as to real meaning on action: the follow through as clear demonstration of not only intent but also continuous action, which is a very powerful force. However, even action may not be enough; it depends on the form that action takes and the degree to which the action is maintained. Lack of maintenance of action will provide space for politicised narratives to gain traction and shape the impact of change agenda through individual reactions. Individual reactions that will manifest politicised conformance, bringing about satisficing behaviour. Such behaviour will maintain the direction of travel of change, but not necessarily to the degree required by management: there will be different layers of change operating at the same points in time through duality of levels of control—organizational and individual, therefore, two forms of collective exercising variable degrees of power.

Narratives, however, shaped through dialogue within formal spaces will shape attitude and behaviour to a much greater degree than through informal spaces because of the inherent power that exist through structure and hierarchy: an inescapable political reality of organizational life that individuals recognise and understand. Conversation will be used to shape and share narratives, therefore, the extent to which formal conversational narratives, and counter-narratives through informal networks (Hyvarinen, 2008), shape change in a politicised sense is an important aspect of power, especially in relation to where power resides; with organization through structured hierarchy or with individuals. Individual internalised conversation (Archer, 2003) provides individuals with power, in that it will determine how they choose to respond and participate in change. This form of power based on reflexive and reflective experiential learning, which if strongly internalised, may create, depending on the nature of proposed changes, a very powerful casus belli to resist change, either actively or passively. Individuals own the degree to which they take an active or passive stance towards formalised change agenda. This creates a duality of control: by organization through management, and individuals in relation to their beliefs and how they shape action relative to self-interest.

Individual internalised dialogue may become open and feed into conversations with colleagues that are trusted, which, depending on the narrative told through conversation, may feed into the general change narrative. This will depend on the personal power that individuals have. The extent to which internal thoughts move from being internalised to open expression within and through formal means will depend on perception, in a political sense, of the extant holding environment. Conversation based on expression of internalised dialogue will also be a reflection of an individual's perception of reality and truth (Le Cornu, 2009), therefore, sharing with selected others who espouse the same sense of reality and truth reinforces extant networks and will also act as a catalyst for extending and creating new networks specific to individuals' change agenda. The content and nature of conversation within networks is not static, conversations will change in relation to stories and narrative threads, and by new information and/or events (McHoul and Rapley, 2001). This does not prevent change from taking place; it does however, shape the degree and depth of change accepted by individuals, and does so through self-interest based conformance dialogue. The use of self-interest based politicised conformance dialogue demonstrates, in one sense, that control of change in a linear sense resides with organizations, even when dialogical approaches are used.

The politics of organizational change is not so much a political ideological struggle, but one focussed on maintaining self-control; it is a way of exercising control over one's true beliefs in relation to one's values (Newman, De Freitas and Knobe, 2014), and, in one sense, to remain free from organizational control through one's beliefs. Sense of freedom within organizations is important for an individual's value of self and place within work, and in relation to organizational performance, especially if creativity and innovation are key elements within an organization's culture. The notion of freedom at work is not a call for total freedom through self-will, which would be a recipe for anarchy that would suit neither individuals nor organization. The link made here is very reminiscent of Mill's (1859) views on liberty entailing the liberty to express one's beliefs in an open way, and being able to do so without incurring the wrath of others and/or alienation. In terms of organizational politics, there being no censure for expressing what one really believes through dialogue within the formal setting. Mill, in relation to the basis for liberty based on personal freedom, argued that views that are counter to the mainstream do not necessarily gain acceptance and place individuals in a position where they either keep quiet, modify their expressed views or openly express what they believe and accept any attendant consequences through their perceived "heresy". This, of course, relates to liberty within society, and does not entirely fit within organization; however, strong parallels exist in terms of where power resides and whether it controls freedom of thought, expression and action. Within organization, there is, of course, a need to be politically astute, which in itself will limit freedom of expression and action. Politicised conformance goes beyond political astuteness and can become part of the very fabric of organization, to such an extent that it "compels" individuals to reduce their own freedom of expression as part of their realpolitik relationship with management, which reinforces conformance—it become a self-fulfilling prophecy that is difficult to break and impossible to remove completely. Political conformance becomes custom, part of the way work is done and the environment within which it takes place; Mill describes such a relationship as the "despotism of custom" which, and this may seem a strong way to express it in terms of organization, is but a form of despotism of political conformance. "Despotism" not in a manufactured sense, but something that comes about through the interaction of individual politicised decision-making based on interpretation—sense of reality—of the prevailing organizational culture and management styles; and managements' inaction in not allowing meaningful debate, challenge, participation etc. All of which will be judged not through rhetoric, but by action.

Of course, some individuals and/or groups will use political power as a form of power projection to protect and/or acquire position; or even use political power for the purpose of sedition—to resist change, to exercise power in a Machiavelli constituent sense, as a reaction to change and its potential impact on an individual's position (Lucchese, 2014). Individuals will think in politically strategic and tactical terms (Vredenburgh and Maurer, 1984), and do so as part of change to try to moderate the impact of change. The reality, however, is that the power of individuals to moderate the impact of change is very limited, which most employees recognise as part of the political reality that exists within organizations—organizational power is represented through structure and resides within and through managerial structures. Individuals will tailor their politicised behaviour to reflect the reality; however, this does not mean that individuals will not aim to exercise what power they have through informal networks. Individuals, based on the political power they may have—formal/informal—will have to decide if they have hard power, soft power, or use political power in a smart way (Wilson, 2008) to affect resistance and/or shape change, either generally and or in relation to specific aspects of change. Informal social networks provide a means by which work is done within organizations (Cross and Parker, 2004) and also provide a framework upon which individuals and groupings can use politics to shape and reinforce both their and others' views out of sight of and between management structures; it is a smart way of exercising political power. Using informal social networks enables individuals and groups to position themselves through using politics and power to advance agenda. Extant social networks and/or ones newly created as a response to change will enable individuals and groups to exercise what power they have, and for the connections to shape formal networks if there are mutual agenda; however, again, such power that is exercised will, in itself, be constrained by the power of organizational conformance requirements. Organizational citizenship behaviour requirements carry its own political tone of conformance, which is part of an individual's and the collective's political reality.

When managing change, organizations make a decision as to how to manage change, in binary terms, either linear or non-linear dialogical approaches. I am not suggesting at this point that the reality involves such a stark choice, in that, change, whether level 1 or level 2, requires structure through planning, even non-linear dialogical approaches. If, for example, we consider the dialogical approach predicated on the power of participative conversation to create openness, transparency and therefore meaningful dialogue as a means to not only reducing possible resistance, but also increasing the level of commitment to the change. A partial challenge to such an approach is to question the degree to which dialogue is open and free of politicised thought and words. In a general sense, the answer depends on authenticity of relationships: trust, respect, rationality etc. However, individuals may still express themselves through politicised language in order, if nothing else, to be polite and not to cause disturbance to their concordat with their line manager and therefore organization. Mulgan's (1974) discusses Aristole's view on "Man" being a political animal as we are social animals—we learn and understand the importance of being politic, which we apply at work through the networks we create and in relation to hierarchy and those that represent it. Politicised language enables employees to conform to organizational, psychological and social contract—one thread connecting all three forms of contract is not to be open about what one really thinks. To be truly open about one's thoughts and beliefs would bring about conflict, which in itself goes against an expected duty to respect others' views; this, of course, does not, exclude robust rational and objective debate.

Politicised language at work as an element of organizational climate, and specifically in relation to organizational change, has greater significance due to the relationship between structure, hierarchy and holding environments. Hierarchy is a constant of organizational life, it is always in place irrespective of the change approach used, it is panoptical in nature and presence, which shapes behaviour and brings conformity through self-administered control, therefore, divesting power to organizations. The degree of panoptical power is not, of course, truly all seeing and physical within organizations, it has a presence that permeates organizational climate, and on the whole is perceived as negative and having a dysfunctional role (Landells and Simon, 2013; Cropanzano, Howes, Grandey and Toth, 1997). Employees make sense, and tend to do so early on when joining an organization, of existing political climates and do so in relation to self. Doing so is part of the social psychology of organizational life within which individuals position themselves (De Cremer, van Dick and Murnighan, 2011). Employees also work out the degree to which it affects the extent to which compliant behaviour shapes relationships through formal and informal networks. However, there are "white spaces" within organizations that are out of view and hidden from managerial gaze, figuratively and literally, and therefore go well beyond managerial control (O'Doherty, Christian De Cock, Rehn and Ashcraft, 2013). Such spaces provide opportunity for narrative to flourish and for key actors that have power to shape the informal dynamic and therefore attitudes to proposed changes.

The extent of employee power has already been discussed; however, it is worth re-emphasising that employees have forms of power and control to a greater extent than is assumed and/or admitted by organizations; power which is unseen and intangible and goes well beyond understanding what motivates individuals, even in relation to transformational or transactional leadership (Timothy and Piccolo, 2004). Organizations adhere to a narrative of change, and one to which employees also adhere in a politicised conformance sense. Individuals, however, control their "true" narrative in relation to how they view change, and do so in relation to their reality of their role within change relative to their interpretation of, meaning and impact of proposed changes. Employees decide how to conform in relation to what they wish to try to hold on to and what they wish to give in a satisficing sense; all elements of which are political decisions that relate to the power that employees have through the psychological contract they wish to create and act upon (Rousseau, 2010) in relation to change. Perversely, a satisficing approach in a politicised sense may satisfy managers, especially if it conforms to an organization's narrative of change: things are changing, and have changed by the due date, so all is as planned, even if in a post-rationalisation sense. Such complex relationships are maintained by the hierarchical positional power that organizations have, and used in an unmanaged way, through structure, hierarchy and delineated control through positional managerial power. For this unspoken, but understood relationship, to work, a form of mutual assured delusion needs to exist and persist, which in itself maintains control; control that suits managerial and non-managerial employees, and maintains a narrative that organizations shape change narratives. Lack of Bohmian dialogue (Bohm, 1996), for example as part of dialogical approaches, maintains the delusion; and breaking the inherent politicised conformance within the narrative resides with employees, irrespective of management's desire to create a more participative polyarchic approach to creating dialogue (Krouse, 1982).

Managers can set the tone of change, but employees own the decision as to the extent to which they participate relative to their self-interest. This, again, takes place within a panoptical environment; panoptical in the sense that employees understand that management gauge—"watch"—degrees of commitment through behaviour and language. Some individuals will see this as an opportunity to actively use their understanding of signalling to demonstrate their commitment to proposed changes in order to create capital (Bliege Bird and Smith, 2005), and do so either in terms of genuine commitment and/or for political expediency reasons. Signalling commitment of support to proposed changes, and through the change process, either based on genuine belief in the proposed changes and/or political positioning in relation to self, can also be viewed in terms of economic contractual signalling (Vasconcelos, 2017), in that, there is possible gain—current or future—to be made by creating political capital through positioning self. It is a way of proving one's worth to an organization through signalling discernible commitment through forms of participation; it is proskynesis in action and behaviour recognised and accepted by managers. It is easier to manage conformance than it is to manage non-conforming employees, generally, and through change. From a managerial perspective, conformance enables change to progress at a set rate, irrespective of what employees actually think, and even how they behave, as the force of proskynesis will, to a large degree, start and maintain change momentum through time related change stages set by management. This, of course, does not have to be the "contractual settlement" from either an organizational or employees' perspective. The point being that organizations, should they wish to base change on meaningful dialogue, need to unsettle the unspoken settlement. To remove, using Mills (1859) term, the "despotism of custom", which is one way of interpreting organizational holding environments, which are not despotic in the true sense of the word, but create, either deliberately or inadvertently, a climate of conformance to power. Managers do not ask employees to perform proskynesis, but through individual experience it becomes the norm and is embedded within change stories, narratives and individual autobiography, the culmination of which is to reduce meaningful dialogue and also to create a self-fulfilling prophecy of change.

The power of politicised conformance behaviour will bring about change, perhaps not to the extent, depth and within the timeframe set by organizations, but change, nevertheless, will take place and generally in line with organizational expectations and goals. Organizational change narratives tend to be, even allowing for a degree of introspection leading to lessons learnt, positive and reinforced by a post-rationalisation of events. Politically, from organizational perspectives, not to have change that is, even allowing for some failures along the way, successful would raise questions on the management of the change process. Successful change will be the narrative, to which employees may well have a counter-narrative, a counter-narrative that remains, depending on the holding environment, unspoken in the general scheme of things, but spoken about through informal networks. This, in itself, creates a new narrative about change experience—individual and collective—that maintains a life of its own that will permeate the fabric of an organization and will shape individual attitudes and behaviour to future change.

This raises the freedom/non-freedom aspect of expressing narrative through dialogical approaches used by organizations. Even though organizations may extol the virtues of dialogue, even to challenge norms through non-conformity, extant holding environments will have shaped employees. Such conditioning is difficult to overcome in order to create meaningful dialogue—*the die is cast*, and recasting it does not necessarily change the outcome in the minds of employees. This, again, is where action is significantly more important than words to begin to try to reshape political relationships between management and employees; and to reframe the degree to which politics shapes interaction and dialogue. This, depending on the degree of distance between organizational narrative and employee counter-narrative, will provide employees with opportunities to re-story their experience to fit their perception of the truth, and a means to counter a reign of silence through structure created by organizational holding environments. The reign of silence will politically dominate the narrative and set the tone for dialogue. Stories will be owned (situated) within individuals and are used to create individual autobiographies (McLean, Pasupathi and Pals, 2007) to shape and justify their stance through and post-change; and are used to share with trusted others within informal spaces to break the formal silence of employees' experience of change.

The power of self-oriented politicised conformance as part of change, and narratives of change, is a powerful force that maintains the shape and direction of change, in that organizations are in control throughout change irrespective of the approach used to manage change. This will also maintain the belief that change, and the inherent decision-making that it involves, is maximising in its orientation. However, the extent to which decision-making on the part of employees is entirely maximising in relation to satisficing behaviour shaped by individual decisions, does not take account of individual degrees of rationality and/or subjectivity, plus political aspects, involved in individual decision-making (Sakhartov and Folta, 2013). The assumption that individuals make decisions in relation to change in a rational objective way is, in terms of self-interest, somewhat delusory; however, as part of organizational stories and narratives of change, decisions are not subjective and do not include self-interest; such stories and narratives have to be maintained in order to maintain the illusion of organizational control. This is the unspoken aspect of organizational dynamics and is dependent on the degree of introspection that organizations wish to undertake (Gover and Duxbury, 2017). It enables organizations to rely on hierrachical power to bring about change in a conformance sense. If this is the case for most organizations, it is in an organization's self-interest to leave politicised conformance unspoken of and in place.

Employee politicised conformance has its own power, but also enhances the power and control that organizations have. As Machiavelli observed in The Prince (Machiavelli, Skinner and Price, 1988), open political behaviour represents rebellion and it disunites the population ("militia" in Machiavelli terms), and therefore increases the power of the aristocracy and/or oligarchy, in the modern sense, management structures and those at the strategic apex of organizations. If this contention is accepted then there is a need to explore: (1) the bases of the symbiotic political relationships that exists within organizational holding environments; (2) how the relationship that exists between formal and informal aspects of organization shape employee engagement within change; (3) the extent to which individual imperatives drive, maintain and constrain change. Chapters Four and Five discuss self-interest based political dimensions of change in more detail.

References

Archer, M. S. (2003) *Structure, Agency and the Internal Conversation*. Cambridge: Cambridge University Press.

Baker, K. A. (2002) *Organizational Communication*. Retrieved June 7, 2009.

Bliege Bird, R. and Smith, E. A. (2005) Signaling Theory, Strategic Interaction, and Symbolic Capital. *Current Anthropology*, 46(2), 221–248.

Bohm, D. (1996). *On Dialogue*. New York: Routledge.

Borgatti, S. P., Mehra, A., Brass, D. J. and Labianca, G. (2009) Network Analysis in the Social Sciences. *Science*, 13, 892–895.

Brass, D. J. and Burkhardt, M. E. (1993) Potential Power and Power Uses: An Investigation of Structure and Behavior. *Academy of Management Journal*, 36(1), 441–470.

Crampton, S. M., Hodge, J. W. and Mishra, J. M. (1998) The Informal Communication Network: Factors Influencing Grapevine Activity. *Public Personnel Management*, 27(4), 569–584.

Cropanzano, R., Howes, J. C., Grandey, A. A. and Toth, P. (1997) The Relationship of Organizational Politics and Support to Work Behaviors, Attitudes, and Stress. *Journal of Organization Behavior*, 18, 159–180.

Cross, R. and Parker, A. (2004) *The Hidden Power of Social Networks: Understanding How Work Really Gets Done in Organization*. Cambridge, MA: Harvard University Press.

De Cremer, D., van Dick, R. and Murnighan, J. K. (eds.) (2011) *Social Psychology of Organizations*. New York: Routledge.

De Dreu, C. K. W. (2004) Rational Self-Interest and Other Orientation in Organizational Behavior: A Critical Appraisal and Extension of Meglino and Korsgaard. *Journal of Applied Psychology*, 91(6), 1245–1252.

De Dreu, C. K. W. and Nauta, A. (2009) Self-Interest and Other-Orientation in Organizational Behavior: Implications for Job Performance, Prosocial Behavior, and Personal Initiative. *Journal of Applied Psychology*, 94(4), 913–926.

Del Lucchese, F. (2014) Machiavelli and Constituent Power: The Revolutionary Foundation of Modern Political Thought. *European Journal of Political Theory*, 16(1), 3–23.

Ford, J. D. (1999) Organizational Change as Shifting Conversations. *Journal of Organizational Change Management*, 12(6), 480–450.

Gover, L. and Duxbury, L. (2017) Making Sense or Organizational Change: I Hindsight 20/20. *Journal of Organizational Behaviour*, 39(1), 39–57.

Harris, S. G. (1994) Organizational Culture and Individual Sensemaking: A Schema-based Perspective. *Organization Science*, 5(3), 309–321.

Herzfeld, M. (2017) Anthropological Realism in a Scientistic Age. *Anthropoloogical Theory*, 18(1), 129–150

Hyvarinen, M. (2008) Analyzing Narratives and Story-Telling. In P. Alasuutari, L. Bickman and J. Brennan (eds.), *The Sage Handbook of Social Research Methods*. London: Sage Publications Ltd.

Krouse, R. (1982) Polyarchy & Participation: The Changing Democratic Theory of Robert Dahl. *Polity*, 14(3), 441–463.

Kurland, N. B. and Hope Pelled, L. (2000) Passing the Word: Toward a Model of Gossip and Power in the Workplace. *Academy of Management*, 25(2), 428–438.

Landells, E. and Albrecht, S. L. (2013) Organizational Political Climate: Shared Perceptions About the Building and Use of Power Bases. *Human Resources Management Review*, 23(4), 357–365.

Le Cornu, A. (2009) Meaning, Internalization, and Externalization Toward a Fuller Understanding of the Process of Reflection and Its Role in the Construction of the Self. *Adult Education Quarterly*, 59(4), 279–297.

Machiavelli, N., Skinner, Q. (ed.), and Price, R. (ed.) (1988) *Machiavelli: The Prince*. Cambridge: Cambridge University Press.

McHoul, A. and Rapley, M. (eds.) (2001) *How to Analyse Talk in Institutional Settings: A Casebook of Methods*. London: Continuum.

McLean, K. C., Pasupathi, M. and Pals, J. L. (2007) Selves Creating Stories Creating Selves: A Process Model of Self-Development. *Personality and Social Psychology Review*, 11(3), 262–278.

Mill, J. S. (1859) *On Liberty*. Reprint, Los Angeles: Enhanced Media Publishing, 2016.

Mulgan, R. G. (1974) Aristotle's Doctrine that Man Is a Political Animal. *Hermes*, 102(3), 438–45.

Newman, G. E., De Freitas, J. and Knobe, J. (2014) Beliefs About the True Self Explain Asymmetries Based On Moral Judgment, *Cognitive Science*, 39, 96–125.

O'Doherty, D., Christian De Cock, C., Rehn, A. and Ashcraft, K. L. (2013) New Sites/Sights: Exploring the White Spaces of Organization. *Organizational Studies*, 34(10), 1427–1444.

Rousseau, D. M. (2010) Schema, Promise and Mutuality: The Building Blocks of the Psychological Contract. *Journal of Occupational and Organizational Psychology*, 74(4), 511–541.

Sakhartov, A. and Folta, T. B. (2013) Rationalizing Organizational Change: A Need for Comparative Testing. *Organization Science*, 24(4), 1140–1156.

Schein, V. E. (1977) Individual Power and Political Behaviors in Organizations: An Inadequately Explored Reality. *Academy of Management Review*, 2(1), 64–72.

Steven Elias, S. (2008) Fifty Years of Influence in the Workplace: The Evolution of the French and Raven Power Taxonomy. *Journal of Management History*, 14(3), 267–283.

Tichy, N. M., Tushman, M. L. and Fombun, C. (1979) Social Network Analysis for Organizations. *The Academy of Management Review*, 4(4), 507–519.

Timothy, J. A. and Piccolo, R. F. (2004) Transformational and Transactional Leadership: A Meta-Analytic Test of Their Relative Validity. *Journal of Applied Psychology*, 89(5), 755–768.

Vasconcelos, L. (2017) A Signalling-based Theory of Contractual Commitment to Relationships. *European Economic Review*, 93, 123–138.

Vredenburgh, D. J. and Maurer, J. G. (1984) A Process Framework of Organizational Politics. *Human Relations*, 37(1) 47–65.

Wilson, III. E. J. (2008) Hard Power, Soft Power, Smart Power. *The ANNALS of the American Academy of Political and Social Science*, 616(1), 110–124.

4 Implications for Managing Change

From an organizational perspective, politicised conformance aids the management of change, and does so irrespective of the approach taken. The power of politicised conformance is not "something done" to employees solely by and through organizational management structures and hierarchy, but is within and through individuals. Individuals do, of course, react to prevailing organizational norms and are shaped, to a lesser or greater extent, by the expectations that organizational norms signal to employees. Employees recognise and understand the need to reflect organizational norms in order to fit-in politically, which is the first layer of politicised conformance that is above the surface: enacted in an open way to management and colleagues, but primarily for the observance of management. The second layer, below the surface, relates to the degree of conformance that individuals decide to exhibit to colleagues: true beliefs, values and norms. There is, therefore, within individuals a duality of conformance based on self-interest that primarily manifests itself to organizations above the surface. This aspect of organizational dynamics, and the dynamics of change, provides organizations, irrespective of any change narrative created by management, the power to manage change primarily through formal power bases inherent within and through structural hierarchy.

Employees understand the reality of power through hierarchy and the extent to which it shapes interactions with hierarchy through management. Employees respond to this reality of organizational life through dialogue, their spoken voice (Islam and Zyphur, 2005). Employees' voice in relation to hierarchical power also shapes the process of organizational change in terms of politicised expectations; expectations that translate into politicised behaviour in order to maintain a form of status quo within formal and informal spaces: role, position, power, networks and so on. (Langley, Smallman, Tsoukas and Van de Ven, 2013). Does this form of unspoken, yet known, power based on politicised conformance enable organizations to maintain linear control oriented approaches to managing change? Many readers will view this question, and what underpins it, as heterodox, and is one that fundamentally challenges the general prevailing views on managing change through people. Managing change, therefore, is not about managing change through people, but one of managing people through change based on degrees of politicised conformance.

Politicised conformance is part of everyday organizational life and change, and goes beyond even evidential bases for determining the true efficacy of dialogical approaches to managing change (Marshak and Grant, 2008). In addition, even if organizations choose to use a dialogical approach to managing change and believe that dialogue facilitated change through employees, the essence of the question is still relevant, in that self-interest based politicised conformance is too powerful for management to overcome through dialogue, even if it is "open dialogue". The proposition at his point is that no dialogue is truly open and therefore free from political thought, thus is not free from politicised conformance. There is a need for managers to acknowledge the power of self-interest and the extent to which it shapes the dynamics of change through not just employee behaviour, but also words. This is not to suggest that self-interest on the part of employees will alter the direction of change, politicised conformance will ensure direction is maintained; but self-interest politicised conformance will determine the degree to which change takes place: temporal and effect on attitude and behaviour, all of which determine change at a deeper level within individuals. It is, as a contention, easier for organizations to assume that managers manage employees through change, but the reality is that employees manage themselves through change in relation to their level of politicised conformance based on self-interest.

If this contention is accepted, then it has significant implications for dialogical approaches to change, in that, if such approaches are to be employed then organizational holding environments need to be reformed through management behaviour in order to *try* to minimise politics within the dynamic. However, political behaviour will never be removed from organizations, as it is us: enlightened self-interest (Dienhart et al., 2001; Firmer and Walker, 2009) may be the best that can be achieved, even if an organizational climate of non-partisan politicised behaviour is the norm. From an organizational perspective, politicised conformance not only aids the management of change, but also brings it about and ensures its "success": "success" in the sense of arriving at a point when management considers the change process is complete.

At this point, it is worth remembering that the power of politicised conformance is something that is not solely "done" to employees by and through organizational hierarchy, but is very much within and through individuals, which gives employees power, too, though not necessarily the same degree of power that can be exercised in an open way through formal spaces. Therefore, change cannot be managed in an absolute control oriented sense because employees exercise politicised power as a counter to the power inherent through hierarchy. Individuals, alongside and within being managed, manage and control themselves through change, therefore, organizations through management structures do not have absolute power and control, and certainly not to the extent they assume they do. Such duality of power, whether in terms of settlement and/or conflict, does not abrogate the formalised power bases inherent within and through structure and concomitant hierarchies (Emerson, 1962; Pfeffer, 1992a). This power dynamic creates a narrative which not only gives meaning to individuals' roles, responsibilities and position, but also their place within the order of things; to primarily be subordinate within structure. Thus, subordination creates a political dynamic that becomes part of the reality of organizational life, therefore significantly shaping employees' perception and sense of reality of where power resides. Individuals' narrative of reality shapes their political selves and relationships with others within and through hierarchy; principally, and in terms of power relationships, an employees' relationship with line management (Mumby, 1987) through degrees of proskynesis.

The reality of management's and employees' mutual understanding of hierarchical power and how it shapes individuals' views of what is required of them in relation to change, manifests itself through political expectations that translate into politicised behaviour in order to maintain a form of settlement for both as to role, position and where power resides. Concomitant with such a view, if one chooses to accept it, is that a well-managed linear approach may be the more realistic and effective, especially set in relation to the temporal aspects of change from an organization's perspective (Bluedorn and Denhardt, 1988); that is, achieving key stages within a change process that signifies movement in a desired direction. Desired direction, that is, from an organization's perspective; a direction that signifies not only movement but also achievement of desired change oriented milestones. This view of change is, as stated, a form of heterodox, if not downright heresy, when stated in relation to extant prevailing views on how to manage change through people based on dialogical approaches (Crestani, 2016 in Simcic Bron, Romenti and Zerfass, 2016; Tonder, 2004). However, the extent to which participative change approaches are effective, outwith a recognition of politicised conformance bringing movement and maintaining the momentum of change, needs to be recognised as a large and distinct element within the reality of change from employees' perspective (Oreg, Michel and Todnem By, 2013). A reality reinforced through structure and hierarchy, irrespective of managerial sensegiving to the contrary.

Managing through unspoken politicised conformance, in essence a linear approach, but doing so in the guise of participative approaches enables organizations to maintain a linear control oriented journey entwined within a dialogical participative narrative. The entwined narratives (Boje, 2012) become a dual reality for managers and non-managerial employees that exerts a power of its own, but primarily through employees' political perspective and conformance. That is not to say that all employees will conform, politicised self-interest based power, of course, can, and does, create resistance, albeit primarily in a *sotto voce* way. If resistance is "quiet" then it remains largely unspoken and does not need managing; individuals manage themselves through change through politicised conformance because it is in their interest to do so. Individuals manage and control this form of settlement, a settlement that resides within them, whilst at the same time also maintaining managerial control. It is a reflection of the reality of position and power: the power that individuals have and own in managing their degree of participation relative to perceived expected conformance, and how they decide to frame their psychological contract in relation to proposed changes. This settlement in action—both sides knowing but not communicating the political dimension, or at the very least being circumspect about it—maintains social co-existence and therefore the unspoken social contract of organizational life: neither side really challenges the accepted power distance aspect of change, even through dialogical approaches to change. The power of a social contract in this form in maintaining and reinforcing holding environments is extensive and deep, unless, of course, employees challenge it in a meaningful open dialogical way expressed through action and not just words. If, on either side, action is not prevalent beyond words then politicised conformance will continue to exist, and does so in such a way that it hampers organizational efficiency and effectiveness, generally, and in relation to change.

The power of self-interest runs deep and drives political thought and action, yet, criticism of organizational politics by employees at all levels tends to blame the "other" for doing it: everyone else is always more political than self! Organizational politics also provides a shield behind which employees can shelter, in that organizational politics can be used to justify non-engagement and/or as a reason for not being able to do get things done. Again, because of the other doing it to me, you and us, which is a way of individuals not recognising and admitting that we are all political at work and the "other" is "us". Organizational politics becomes, in the minds of employees, a valid rational reason for disengaging, or not fully engaging, generally and in relation to change, beyond politicised signalling through words and actions of conformance. If this view is accepted, then there are multiple strands to organizational social contracts (Keeley, 1980), which means that organizations will have a view of—choose to assume—what the organizational social contract is; however, so do employees have a view, a view that may run counter and/or contradict the organizational view. This, in itself, creates conflict of varying degrees within and between individuals, and in relation to organizational agenda.

Lack of meaningful dialogue that fully recognises the self-interest and the politics of context will keep the assumed and unspoken organizational contract in place. If this relationship remains unspoken, it will get in the way of engaging employees through dialogue as part of managing change. The uncertainty inherent within change (Shaw, 2002) persists at a deeper level than otherwise assumed, and individuals going through change may be doing so in a superficial way based on self-interest based politicised conformance. This creates a dual-narrative—organizational narrative that change is happening and through dialogue if dialogical approaches are used; but on the other hand the narrative of employees will be one of we have to go along with the change irrespective of any dialogue as part of participative change. The result of this is that change happens, and employees will change, but not for the reasons espoused through any organizational narrative that claims that change was through employees' participation and dialogue. If this is the case, then the delusion of change through and by employees becomes a reinforcing narrative, and so the social remains contract is intact; all is calm above the surface.

Part of the mantra of managing change is that it is complex, which indeed it is, but needs to be viewed as layered complexity, in that some aspects can be managed and many cannot. For example, understanding the role of effective communication in order to understand employee views, issues, concerns etc. to avoid misinterpretation in order to create meaningful dialogue. However, the role of effective communication as part of change is well understood (Finbarr, Teague and Kitchen, 2003), though not necessarily well practised. It is an aspect that is more nuanced and more difficult to get to grips with, especially the political dimension to words and associated actions, including silence in the literal sense and through non-engagement (Ng and Bradac, 1995). For managers to try and manage the political dimension of communication requires good relational management skills and the creation of a safe space within which employees can express themselves freely, which will, from a management perspective, create a higher degree of uncertainty due to what may be discussed. Increased uncertainty has to be accepted and facilitated through creating spaces of "safe uncertainty" (Mason, 2015) within which, ideally, all employees can discuss not just their rational response to change but also their emotional response, both elements of which will frame the politicised dimension in relation to politicised conformance. The aim being, to de-politicise the workplace environment

(Flinders and Buller, 2006), to reduce its effect on shaping interactions, communication, and forming deeper and more open relationships between management and non-managerial employees.

Creating a space free—or at least freer—of politics is quite a tall order, even within organizations that already have more inclusive and participative-based management styles that welcome and encourage engagement. The reality is that no organization can ever be free of politics and self-interest as it comes not just from the holding environment shaped and/or reinforced through individual managers, but comes directly from individuals. The implications of this is not to suggest there needs to be a free-for-all through dialogue, and that hierarchy, for example, needs to be subverted: the reality of hierarchy through structure needs to be in place in order for most organizations to function, and employees look for both to fulfil their sense of place, role, responsibilities, self-worth and so on. So what is required, what needs to be in place in order to try to de-politicise, in a reductive sense, the workplace? In short, action is needed, not just rhetoric, to avoid simulacrum, that is, an image that represents something, with the operative words being "image" and "representation". Words alone do not create a safe space, in fact, rhetoric alone will reinforce politicised conformance because inaction from words becomes part of a reinforcing narrative. Individuals see beyond rhetoric, and do so very quickly: we see words alone as mere "puff", to use a legal term, but one that is very apt in this instance.

If organizations wish to create safe spaces for open and challenging dialogue then managers must follow through with action. Action—*the words that never lie*—alongside words must permeate an organization, from strategic apex down to operational level so that a new political dynamic and narrative can be created through symbolic action (Hallett, 2003). To do this, action must begin at senior management level, very quickly followed by enaction through middle management down to and through supervisory levels; this, of course, takes place within structure, hierarchy and culture that will still hold employees in a form of stasis until things are seen to be different. This view is not new, in fact, it is restating the obvious; however, embedded within this approach should be enactivism, which addresses the relationship between individual autonomy and the degree to which behaviour is socially patterned (Baerveldt and Verheggen, 1999).

In order to begin to change organizational politicals as part of the dynamic of culture, and to do so through enactivism and dialogue, there is a need to understand the degree to which politicised behaviour is either purely self-interest driven or is a manifestation of cultural patterns being observed and enacted by employees. Understanding the drivers of politicised behaviour will not provide an absolute answer in itself, especially in relation to self-interest. To restate a point already made, and an obvious one, ownership of self resides completely within individuals; individuals have the final say irrespective of external forces in terms of belief, thought, emotion, rationality and action. Understanding enactivism (Sridharan, 2015) however may enable new patterns of behaviour to be set that encourages employees to feel free to enter into dialogue without conscious awareness of having to be political in thought, speech and action. Such freedom will shape individual internalised beliefs, and may do so to such an extent that internal thought becomes externalised, and not just in words, but also through action. The benefits of this to organizational performance and change are, in many ways, obvious; however, from an individual perspective it can affect motivation through higher levels of self-esteem, self-efficacy, locus of control, and emotional stability (Judge and Bono, 2001), all of which enhance individual performance and therefore that of organizations. Specific to managing change, higher levels of motivation, emotional stability, self-esteem and control all have potential to have a high positive impact on managing change through employee engagement; engagement that would be at a higher emotional ownership level and therefore deeper in terms of embedding change within and through individuals. It creates higher levels of psychological capital and emotions within individuals at all levels within an organization (Avey, Wernsing and Luthans, 2008), and stronger more meaningful psychological contracts.

Politicised thought and action relates very much to the four aspects listed, in that, individuals will, through their ownership of thought and action, not necessarily have to compromise what they really think and believe. Individuals will feel genuinely empowered through freedom of speech, which will help individuals transition through change in a less painful way, depending, of course, on what the nature of change is. This is not a panacea to managing change, as self-interest in a change equation sense (Balogun and Hope Hailey, 2004) will still be a powerful force in determining an individual's reaction to change: this aspect of change will never be eliminated and will in many ways be beyond managing; it is part of the reality in a realpolitik sense. This deeper approach has potential to have a significant positive impact on organizational culture based on meaningful engagement on the part of all employees. It also has potential significance in terms of managing change if a more employee-centred approach is used, that is, being able to use dialogical approaches within cultures that are freer, though not completely free, of politicised behaviour and conformance, there being significantly more meaningful involvement on the part of employees to drive and bring about change.

At senior management levels there needs to be action through visibility in order to set an appropriate tone to create a climate that encourages open dialogue (Mazutis and Slawinski, 2008). Senior management must go well beyond exhortations through briefings; they must go beyond rhetoric. Again, actions will speak louder, if not volumes, about real intent. If senior managers state something along the lines of "I have an open door; let me know what you think etc.., then they must follow through; they must demonstrate leadership in order to foster an inclusive approach and therefore welcome involvement form employees so that they have a voice that is recognised and listened to" (Boekhorst, 2015). Lack of follow through will create a narrative that will shape behaviour through enactivism, in that individuals will decide for themselves and among themselves to behave in a way that reflects their reality. Words alone will not create a new narrative, so if senior management wish to create a culture of inclusion through depoliticsing climate and therefore behaviour, they have no alternative but to engage through visible actions (Niehoff, Enz and Grover, 1990; Sarros, Cooper and Santora, 2008; Belios and Koustelios, 2014).

The same principles apply to middle line management, which will require managers to demonstrate the same degree of leadership by creating stronger, more meaningful relations (Walumbwa and Hartnell, 2011) with subordinates in order to shape individual behaviour and performance within a freer political climate. At the operational level, supervisory staff and subordinate employees also need degrees of freedom to engage in a de-politicised way. Again, elements of leadership, or better relational management, are needed in order to reinforce tone through climate into culture to bring about organizational citizenship behaviours based on stronger relational bonds (Wang, Law, Hackett, Wang and Chen, 2005) that help to mitigate politicised behaviour.

Social patterns within organizations, of course, will shape attitude and behaviour based on individuals' observations, interpretation and inclination towards the nature and role of politics within organizations, and do so in relation to the nature of proposed changes relative to self (Oreg, 2006).

It needs to be remembered that social patterns are created and therefore owned by the society, or mostly by those within society that have power to shape, which applies equally within organizations; however, it should also not be forgotten that structure and work routine will also create social patterns. Therefore, when thinking in terms of social patterns within organizational culture, there is a need to interpret social patterns in the same way as organizational culture, that is, multi-faceted and layered, which adds to the degree of complexity. Complexity that makes managing in a totally control oriented way impossible, but not unmanageable through tone created through action oriented management. The owners of the patterns, of course, will be those actors and actants that have personal power. The degree to which observable patterns bring about forms of proskynesis will be determined by the extent to which politicised conformance is required in relation to an individual's desire to maintain autonomy based on individual values and norms set in terms of proposed changes.

However, even if an individual wishes to maintain their individuality and autonomy through change, they will still have to conform to organizational requirements. This, depending on the nature of the change and the degree to which an organization nullifies an individual's concerns about the change, will shape an individual's psychological contract (van den Heuval and Schalk, 2009), though not to the extent that an individual becomes depoliticised. The political dimension will remain, but may manifest itself in a different way and have a different locus. Again, the realpolitik of organizational life is one of conformity, or at least degrees of conformity, recognition of which demonstrates understanding of the realities of where ultimate control lies, that is, within hierarchy. Individuals will conform to the "rules of the game", even if there is a desire to resist change (an interesting counter-view to using the term "resistance to change" can be found in Dent and Galloway Goldberg, 1998). Resistance will take a politicised form, in Machiavelli's term, to become a "partisan"—an individual, who on the surface may be conforming, but resisting through inner-self etc.., and/or resisting through action. Action in this sense refers to utilising what power an individual has to create support, either to resist and block changes in order to mitigate the impact of proposed changes on self in terms of routine and work-patterns, and/or to create a support network comprising like-minded others.

To begin to set new social patterns through action, the role of management, as already stated, through visibility and demonstrating attributes such as co-operation, trust, mutual respect etc. is key (Ghoshal and Bartlett, 1994). And not only in relation to change, but through setting a tone that persists post-change, especially if an organization wishes to create a learning and change oriented culture based on dialogue that is more open (Scott, Cook and Yanow, 1993). This requires leadership from the top of an organization, with a key role for senior management teams to demonstrate commitment through taking an active and continuous lead and not just leave it to meso level managers and below to implement after any initial exhortations (Dusya and Crossan, 2004). However, management must also recognise that their power to reduce the extent of proskynesis is limited, it is employees who will determine the impact of new de-politicised dialogue; employees will decide and own the decision to accept or reject. This provides employees with power, albeit tempered by politicised conformance, to shape not just their reaction through acceptance or rejection, but also that of others, including managers. If employees decide not to engage then extant ways of doing things in a politicised sense will not change— employees will have decided to retain their status quo with managers and therefore the organization.

How senior managers, and management per se, communicate is key to trying to shape employees in readiness for change through dialogue. The language used, and how it should shape follow-on actions, needs to be given very careful consideration in order to avoid ambiguity of intentions. Management will need to move beyond just relying on briefings, question and answer sessions and the like; all of which will have a distinct and clear role to play. Managers charged with taking a lead role in change will need to think about how they use language in an intentional performative way. The use of language in this way is paramount to beginning to shape attitude and thus behaviour through change in order to have effect (Ford and Ford, 1995). Performative linguistics goes beyond using words from the "managing change lexicon" to using linguistics based on a clear recognition and understanding of how language shapes attitude and behaviour to change, especially if language is to change the social reality of a context.

In the case of the political dimension to change, and in relation to politicised conformance, directly linking actions through the words used is a fundamental part of dialogical approaches to change. A form of managing change that can be more effective if managers have the requisite skills, time and emotional intelligence to manage employees through using language in a different way from that which may be the norm on a day-to-day basis. Ideally, this approach to using language in a more focussed and effective way should begin before any change programme begins, again, and especially, if an organization wishes to create a culture that is outward looking, learning based and change oriented. This does not mean that performative linguistic approaches, if not already in place, cannot be used, but if it is to be used then it needs to be given more prominence when planning for change and individual managers will need to appraise how they communicate and how they will need to change their use of language.

In conclusion, understanding the complexity of self-interest politicised conformance enables organizations to understand the "unspoken" political nature of employees' attitudes and behaviour way, generally, and in relation to change (Pfeffer, 1992b). The general context will always shape the change context, so participative approaches to managing change will be essentially linear control oriented if the holding environment is not fully analysed to include the political dimension and the extent to which it shapes employees in a symbiotic relational sense. In addition, employees fully understand the political dimension inherent within change and the power that it provides them with, and they understand how to exercise such politicised power in relation to self and preserving, or trying to preserve, those aspects of how they wish to continue to do the work. Individuals, even if safe space exists, will still make decisions that will incorporate a self-interest based dimension and it will shape words and actions. For individuals not to do so would mean an abandonment of a form of power they have control over and can use.

If this contention is accepted then it has significant implications for managing change, in that organizations have a lot of unspoken power through politicised conformance that will act as a driver of change, but employees also have power through their self-interest based politicised power they may choose to exercise. This creates dissonance between employees and organizational change objectives and within individuals, which individuals will reconcile, and not management; however, the reality of the matter is that overarching power resides with organizations reflected in politicised conformance, ergo, if an organization decides to change, the change will happen. In addition, if change, to a degree, is self-managed then does this mean that change frameworks as employed by organizations are nothing more than a form of window dressing? Organizations are not democracies and employees know that they do not have liberty to express freely their views. So even the concept of safe spaces for de-politicised dialogue will not fundamentally change how individuals behave at work. This creates an understanding of constrained freedom—Burkean Paine dichotomy—of action and expression, even when dialogical approaches are used. Employees know that their voice is limited in its effect, which reinforces the need to be circumspect at best with words and actions based on self-interest.

References

Avey, J. B., Wernsing, T. S. and Luthans, F. (2008) Can Positive Employees Help Positive Organizational Change? Impact of Psychological Capital and Emotions on Relevant Attitudes and Behaviors. *The Journal of Applied Behavioral Science*, 44(1), 48–70.

Baerveldt, C. and Verheggen, T. (1999) Enactivism and the Experiential Reality of Culture: Rethinking the Epistemological Basis of Cultural Psychology. *Culture & Psychology*, 5(2), 183–206.

Balogun, J. and Hope Hailey, V. (2004) *Exploring Strategic Change* (2nd ed.). Harlow: Financial Times/Prentice Hall.

Belios, D. and Koustelios, A. (2014) The Impact of Leadership and Change on Organizational Culture. *European Scientific Journal*, 10(7), 451–470.

Bluedorn, A. C. and Denhardt, R. B. (1988) Time and Organizations. *Journal of Management*, 14(2), 299–320.

Boekhorst, J. A. (2015) The Role of Authentic Leadership in Fostering Workplace Inclusion: A Social Information Processing Perspective. *Human Resource Management*, 54(2), 241–264.

Boje, D. M. (2012) Quantum Physics of Storytelling. *Journal of Change Management*, 12, 252–271.

Crestani, I. (2016) Change Communication: Emerging Perspectives for Organisations and Practitioners, in (ed.) *The Management Game of Communication, Advances in Public Relations and Communication Management*, 1, 225–244.

Dent, E. B. and Galloway Goldberg, S. (1998) Challenging "Resistance to Change". *The Journal of Applied Behavioral Science*, 35(1), 25–41.

Dienhart, J., Dennis Moberg, D. and Ron Duska, R. (eds.). (2001) *The Next Phase of Business Ethics: Integrating Psychology and Ethics* (Research in Ethical Issues in Organizations, Volume 3). Bingley, UK: Emerald Group Publishing Limited, 193–210.

Dusya, V. and Crossan, M. (2004) Strategic Leadership and Organizational Learning. *Academy of Management Review*, 29(2), 222–240.

Emerson, R. (1962) Power-Dependence Relations. *American Sociological Review*, 27(1), 31–41.

Finbarr, D., Teague, P. and Kitchen, P. (2003) Exploring the Role of Internal Communication During Organizational Change. *Corporate Communications: An International Journal*, 8(3), 153–162.

Flinders, M. and Buller, J. (2006) Depoliticisation: Principles, Tactics and Tools. *British Politics*, 1, 293–318.

Ford, D. and Ford, L. W. (1995) The Role of Conversations in Producing Intentional Change in Organizations. *Academy of Management Review*, 20(3), 541–570.

Frimer, J. and Walker, A. (2009) Reconciling the Self and Morality: An Empirical Model of Moral Centrality Development. *Developmental Psychology*, 45(6), 1669–1681.

Ghoshal, S. and Bartlett, C. A. (1994) Linking Organizational Context and Managerial Action: The Dimensions of Quality of Management. *Strategic Management*, 15(S2), 91–112.

Hallett, T. (2003) Symbolic Power and Organizational Culture. *Sociological Theory*, 21(2), 128–149.

Islam, G. and Zyphur, M. J. (2005) Power, Voice, and Hierarchy: Exploring the Antecedents of Speaking Up in Group. *Group Dynamics: Theory, Research, and Practice*, 9(2), 93–103.

Judge, T. A. and Bono, J. E. (2001) Relationship of Core Self-Evaluations Traits—Self-Esteem, Generalized Self-Efficacy, Locus of Control, and Emotional Stability—With Job Satisfaction and Job Performance: A Meta-Analysis. *Journal of Applied Psychology*, 86(1), 80–92.

Keeley, M. (1980) Organizational Analogy: A Comparison of Organismic and Social Contract Models. *Administrative Science Quarterly*, 25(2), 337–362.

Langley, A., Smallman, C., Tsoukas, H. and Van de Ven, A. H. (2013) Process Studies of Change in Organization and Management: Unveiling Temporality, Activity, and Flow. *Academy of Management Journal*, 56(1), 1–13.

Marshak, R. J. and Grant, D. (2008) Organizational Discourse and New Organization Development Practices. *British Journal of Management*, 19, S7–S19.

Mason, B. (2015) Towards Positions of Safe Uncertainty. *InterAction—The Journal of Solution Focus in Organizations*, 7(1), 28–43.

Mazutis, D. and Slawinski, N. (2008) Leading Organizational Learning Through Authentic Dialogue. *Management Learning*, 39(4), 437–456.

Mumby, D. K. (1987) The Political Function of Narrative in Organizations. *Communication Monographs*, 54(2), 113–127.

Ng, S. H. and Bradac, J. J. (1995) Power in Language: Verbal Communication & Social Influence // Review. *Canadian Journal of Communication*, 20(2), 278–280.

Niehoff, B. P., Enz, C. A. and Grover, R. A. (1990) The Impact of Top-Management Actions on Employee Attitudes and Perceptions. *Group & Organization Management*, 15(3), 337–352.

Oreg, S. (2006) Personality, Context, and Resistance to Organizational Change. *European Journal of Work and Organizational Psychology*, 15(1), 73–101.

Oreg, S., Michel, A. and Todnem By, R. (2013) *The Psychology of Organizational Change Viewing Change From the Employee's Perspective*. Cambridge: Cambridge University Press.

Pfeffer, J. (1992a) *Managing With Power Politics and Influence in Organizations*. Boston: Harvard Business School Press.

Pfeffer, J. (1992b) Understanding Power in Organizations. *California Management Review*, 34(2), 29–51.

Sarros, J. C., Cooper, B. K. and Santora, J. C. (2008) Building a Climate for Innovation Through Transformational Leadership and Organizational Culture. *Journal of Leadership & Organizational Studies*, 15(2), 145–158.

Scott, D., Cook, N. and Yanow, D. (1993) Culture and Organizational Learning. *Journal of Management Inquiry*, 2(4), 373–390

Shaw, P. (2002) *Changing Conversations in Organizations: A Complexity Approach to Change*. London: Routledge.

Simcic Brønn, P., Romenti, S. and Ansgar Zerfass, A. (eds.) (2016) *The Management Game of Communication* (Advances in Public Relations and Communication Management, Volume 1). Bingley, UK: Emerald Group Publishing Limited, 225–244.

Sridharan, V. (2015) Beyond Consensual Domains: Enactivism, Social Representations and Third-Order Unities. *Culture & Psychology*, 21(2), 259–275.

Tonder, C. (2004) Exploring the Nature of Nonlinear Organizational Change: A Case Study of a "Run-on-Deposits". *Emergence: Complexity and Organization*, 8(1), 30–41.

van den Heuval, S. and Schalk, R. (2009) The Relationship Between Fulfilment of the Psychological Contract and Resistance to Change During Organizational Transformations. *Social Science Information*, 48(2), 283–313.

Walumbwa, F. O. and Hartnell, C. A. (2011) Understanding Transformational Leadership—Employee Performance Links the Role of Relational Identification and Self-Efficacy. *Journal of Occupational and Organizational Psychology*, 84(1), 153–172.

Wang, H., Law, K. S., Hackett, R. D., Wang, D. and Chen, Z. X. (2005) Leader-Member Exchange as a Mediator of the Relationship Between Transformational Leadership and Followers' Performance and Organizational Citizenship Behavior. *Academy of Management Journal*, 48(3), 420–432.

5 Managing the Political and Power Dynamic of Change

As this is the final chapter, it is worth reminding ourselves that given the inherent complexity of organizational politics through individuals, there is no straightforward solution to managing the political and power dynamics of change; perhaps, and at best, we should think in terms of managing through the milieu. A milieu that requires managers to think and behave in a different way, a different way that, at the very least, recognises that power, a key constituent of organizational politics, is located throughout organizations well beyond what hierarchies define through position, and that employees are able to exercise power through change in a way that reflects self-interest agenda. Individuals, in one sense, behave in a Hobbesian (1588–1679, 1651) way that maintains the "articles of peace" in order to avoid "disturbance of the commonwealth", thus avoiding, to varying degrees, disturbance to individuals' and their sense of commonwealth.

Seeing organizations as a form of commonwealth helps us to understand the conflicting forces at play based on individual employee relationships with organization, others and self. Individuals reconcile within themselves the range and meaning of relationships. However, a key part of the reconciliation is in relation to self, that is, to be at peace with oneself based on a desire to be at peace with others, including organization, generally and in a political sense. Individuals, as part of inner peace—an internal rational-emotional settlement in one sense—and in relation to a conscious settlement within organization, recognise a need to accept that in order to have a settlement there needs to be political peace, at least outwardly through politicised conformance. Individuals recognise that too much overt political behaviour disturbs the peace; however, this does not mean there is no disturbance below the surface. Individuals make and take decisions that maintain the peace in politicised conformance that is above the surface, but below the surface, are far more prepared to be a part of disturbance if it fits their agenda.

The importance of organizational culture in determining efficiency, effectiveness, creativity and innovation is a core element within the "modern management mantra", at the centre of which is the importance of employees: "our most valuable asset" aspect of the mantra. In addition, there are numerous texts on organizational politics, usually expressed in terms of "how to play the political game". However, what they rarely do is to recognise the extent and significant role that self-interest plays in shaping attitude and behaviour as part of organizational politics through conformance and therefore organizational performance, generally and in relation to change. The issue, therefore, for organizations is one of creating a different form of "commonwealth" through reframing control, power and the "laws" of political behaviour; a commonwealth that actively encourages individuals through enactivism on the part of management to speak their mind without fear. A commonwealth that creates meaningful political liberty for all employees, and at all levels, as part of organizational citizenship behaviour through reframing organizational social contracts. In addition, and within this, organizations need to accept more disturbance above the surface in order to try to minimise disturbance below the surface to create and maintain a healthy peace through open and challenging discussion. Mill, in *On Liberty* (1859), stated, in relation to personal freedom within a state, that deviation is impious; in an organizational sense, it is considered impious to be non-conformist, generally and in a politicised sense, and is seen as breaking the peace of the commonwealth, the social order, even. Therefore, if there is to be greater political freedom within organizations through dialogical based managerial approaches as part of a permissive culture then individuals who deviate through challenge need to be seen as enhancing organizational performance and not as "impious" employees.

This chapter will therefore focus on reframing self-interest in relation to the role of management within more polyarchic oriented organizational cultures (Golsorkhi, Courpasson and Sallaz, 2012) as a means of mitigating politicised conformance. In addition, if organizations are to manage change through participative dialogical approaches, there is a need for them to shape organizational dynamics through setting a tone that becomes a strong antithesis to politics and politicking. Politicised conformance within change dynamics, of course, does not operate within a vacuum, therefore, extant holding environments cannot be ignored in terms of the extent to which organizational dynamics shapes pre-change narratives and therefore individuals' perception through into action and/or inaction. However, managers should bear in mind that organizations do not have absolute control over employees: employees own their inner-self and behaviour (Hesson and Olpin, 2013), therefore, attempting to shape dynamics as if in a vacuum is a mistake as the organizational psychological space is not "owned" by managers and therefore not totally owned by organization. If employees are to participate in change they need to be allowed and encouraged to find their authentic voice, one that is free of political sensitivities and replication of organizational rhetoric, and be encouraged to do so as part of daily interaction in order for it to be part and parcel of change: before, during and after the event. Organizations, in order to reduce the dysfunctional aspects of the political tension and conflict inherent within change need to be more open politically as part of polyarchic orientation, especially if change is to be deeper and sustainable beyond the initial flurry of activity that is usually associated with change initiatives. To reiterate, managers at the strategic apex, alongside line managers, have a crucial role to play in setting such a non-politicised tone. Without this, and undertaken with real meaning, employees will remain fixed within their stories and narratives of organizational change and organizational politics.

What we learn, generally and in a politicised sense, through socialisation within organizations is a form of proskynesis enactment that reduces the propensity for openness, honesty, meaningful debate etc., and gets in the way of creating a meaningful learning-based organizational culture. Employees become part of a process of organizational political acculturation, which in turn becomes part a political and managerial narrative (Boje, 2012); narratives which are of the past and which run into, and shape, the current and future narratives. The symbiosis of past, current and future is largely determined through individual and collective retrospective sensemaking (Weick, 1995), so part of making sense of the way that holding environments shape political dynamics also needs to be taken into account by managers. Individuals need to be at the centre (McGuire and Hutchings, 2006) in order to begin to understand and therefore facilitate a change in holding environments. This requires action beyond rhetoric in order to mitigate retrospective aspects of sensemaking in order to shape the current and future orientation of employees. It also requires a reduction of politicised conformance in order to shape and maintain organizational citizenship behaviour (Vigoda-Gadot and Drory, 2006) that maintains "peace of the commonwealth", but at the same time liberates individuals from politicised conformance in relation to power and control through hierarchy.

If action beyond rhetoric is used to reduce politicised conformance, and is successful, then individuals may begin to rethink the degree to which political influence (Christiansen, Villanova and Mikulay, 1997) is necessary to affect and shape others, including influencing how they are viewed by managers relative to an organization's political climate. To this end, and as previously stated, organizations need to change their holding environments (Buskirk and McGrath, 1999) and the constructs that maintain hierarchy and concomitant socio-political order, otherwise trying to create a new climate just based on rhetoric will, at best, have marginal impact, or at worst, fail: organizations remain in a condition of politicised conformance stasis. Baum (1989) argued that there is a need for a more sophisticated approach to understanding organizational politics, especially in order to create good constitutions for the common good. Constitutions for the common good, equitable with the notion of commonwealth and peace, within which individuals have greater meaningful centrality, and have a voice that is unadulterated through politicised conformance.

Stronger constitutions based on polyarchic principles, within which individuals' voices are recognised and listened to, create a strong foundation upon which to build and develop healthy climates that bring about improved individual and collective performance as part of learning based cultures through into change. This approach reduces the dysfunctional aspects of organizational politics that get in the way of dialogical approaches to change. It encourages and facilitates the functional aspects; functional through negotiation as part of organizational diplomacy, and recognises self-interest for what it is, in that it is always present, but does not have to get in the way, not in totality, of the common good. Reshaping organizational holding environments in line with what is proposed will require individuals within hierarchy to move away from having concern for maintenance of position and power in a self-interested way. This does not mean that hierarchy is replaced and or necessarily undermined, but is deformed in order to encourage reduced politicised thinking and behaviour conformance. Such a change will require managers, at all levels, to minimise their self-interest as part of decision-making in order to set a de-politicised tone; a tone that must have meaning and not just a disguised form of politicised conformance on their part based on fear of not having a role and place within hierarchy. If such fear exists and persists then managers will play a game of politicised conformance through hierarchy that subordinates will very quickly ascertain, which will then bring about politicised conformance on their part, thus politicised conformance stasis ensues.

Further to conformance to hierarchy as part of structure, Luke (1974) refers to organizational structure being composed of three dimensions: subjective interests; observable conflict in relation to current and potential issues; and political decision-making and control over agenda. Alongside this are the rational-emotional aspects of employees (Sheard, Kakabadse and Kakabadse, 2011). Managing these elements, and the strong forces inherent within, is quite a tall order, but needs to be part of the reality of the difficulty of the task. Modification of behaviours to fit new organizational citizenship behaviours within a redefined "commonwealth" becomes key, in that individuals will need to rebalance approach in order to create a new relationship between involvement/non-involvement, emotional engagement and/or emotional disengagement. Dialogical change, for it to work to the degree it offers, requires a balanced rational-emotional-engagement relationship on the part of individuals with organizational goals. This can only come about if politicised behaviour is minimised; it can only be minimised, and not eradicated due to self-interest being a dominant force within individuals.

Managers and those with leadership power within hierarchy, therefore, have a clear and crucial role in setting an appropriate tone, part of which will be about addressing forms of control and the degree to which hierarchy is maintained and/or reformed. Control mechanisms are a potent force that maintain stasis conditions within organizations and thus prevent effective relational management and/or leadership from taking place, at least in a shared sense, and from changing organizational control mechanisms. In addition, employees, through a new managerial tone, must be encouraged to become free from command and control (Seddon, 2005) in order to bring about a change in politicised attitude, thus bringing about a change in general attitude and behaviour, individually and collectively through shaping, influencing and challenging prevailing organizational norms in order to achieve organizational effectiveness. The purpose of this is not to undermine hierarchy and/or the role of management or those in leadership positions, but to reshape the political aspects of organizational holding environments in relation to individual perception and the degree of politicised conformance that is expected. Reshaping holding environments requires a fundamental rethinking of: (1) Institutional logics (Besharov and Smith, 2014; Greenwood et al., 2010); (2) Rituals (Tilesik, 2010); (3) Ceremony (Meyer and Rowan, 1977); (4) Core symbols (semiotics) (Friedland and Alford, 1991; Stapley, 1996); (5) Emotion (Calhoun, 2001; Toubiana and Zietsma, 2017); and (6) Behaviour (Stapley, 1996). These aspects do, of course, encompass the complexity of institutions (Delbridge and Edwards, 2013; Smets and Jarzabkowski, 2013) and are key to understanding the role that politics and politicised conformance plays in organizational life, especially in relation to the way power manifests itself through politicised conformance behaviour.

Furthermore, seeing organization from an anthropological perspective provides a more nuanced view of the socio-cultural aspects, for example, linguistics, which, as discussed previously, plays an elemental role within change narratives and politics. The extent to which managers and/or leaders can manage through such complexity is, of course, a key aspect of organizational life and managing change. This also challenges the extent to which senior management is prepared to contest command and control oriented organizational holding environments in terms of social architecture and socio-political constructs in order to reach into the very core of an organization and avoid inertia (Kelly and Amburgey, 1991;

Hannan,and Freeman, 1984). These become the precepts for facilitating a different management approach and, ideally, coalescing around those managers that have the requisite relational and leadership attributes and skills to set a new tone through action that is enlivens dialogue, learning and change.

The answer, in the eyes of some, is leadership or a form of managerial leadership as the means to enhance organizational performance (Burgoyne, Hirsh and Williams, 2004); however, before this premise is accepted, a number of fundamental elements need consideration.

First, if "leadership" is just a symbolic word used in place of management to create the notion of doing things differently—the word is different but the function is the same—then it will have little or no impact beyond micro levels. Second, the extent to which organizations fully understand the implications of using the word "leadership" and their preparedness to reassess organizational control mechanisms to alter the power balance in order for leadership and/or management, as it is frequently advocated, to revitalise organizational climate and political discourse through action. Moreover, organizations frequently require managers to take a lead without any meaningful attempt made to change organizational holding environments (Gould, Stapely and Stein, 2006). This creates a dilemma in terms of organizational expectations set against what managers and/or leaders have the freedom to do in order to encourage debate that is more meaningful and challenging as a means of encouraging functional deviancy in order to avoid politicised conformance as part of change. To do so may challenge hierarchy and attendant power-balance relationships, but is essential if open discussion as part of organizational climate is to take place. To reiterate, this does not undermine hierarchy, but reforms it through setting a de-politicised tone and narrative through different actions and behaviour on the part of management. This requires organizations to have a greater appreciation of managerial realism (Reed, 2005) in their assessment of the impact of leadership, and to reassess the value placed on effective line management's impact on improving employee performance and engagement on a day-to-day basis. Management does not have to be a grand philosophy, rather, it is about fundamental interactions between managers and subordinates as they occur "in the moment" and on a day-to-day basis (Kouzes and Posner, 2007). The importance of these interactions is not the sole preserve of leadership, but relates to working manager–employee relationships within hierarchy; the day-to- day interactions set the tone and thus shape attitude and behaviour. If organizations really desire leadership at all levels, giving serious and meaningful consideration to releasing management and employees from their psychological prisons (Morgan, 2006; Oswick and Jones, 2006) of hierarchical cultures that still predominate within organizations is key.

In order to reshape holding environments so as to remove psychological political prisons created by the interplay between holding environments and self-interested politicised behaviour, there is a base requirement for organizations to open the cell doors to allow freedom within which employees feel safe to discuss issues above, and not below, the surface of organizational life. The key elements are:

- Leadership capacity
- Strong managerial relations
- Shared and individual responsibility
- Clear objectives but no micro-management
- Accepting and dealing with risk
- Sharing resources
- Sharing ideas
- Shared timely decision-making
- Challenging norms
- Continuous development
- Addressing challenges

To be successful across these elements and in order to avoid a form of conformance groupthink that creates a delusion of openness and dialogue (Bénabou, 2009), organizations will need to have managers and/or leaders that not only understand themselves, but also the role that self-interest based politicised conformance plays in shaping relations. In addition, and of equal importance, the need to adopt a more realistic approach to accepting that power is diffuse and diffused throughout organizations and also resides within individuals. A form of power that cannot always be accessed and or redirected, especially if the nature of change is one that challenges those things that individuals wish to hang on to: the change equations aspect. Specifically relating this to managing change, those tasked with taking a lead will need to:

- Model the way—align words, narrative and actions with shared expectations and values;
- Create common vision through shared aspirations based on open dialogue and action;
- Allow and enable employees to challenge processes at all levels— experiment, take risks, innovate etc.;
- Enable employees to act—build political trust, political freedom to act, develop competence to act; and
- Encourage employees—recognise contributions and show appreciation, celebrate success (spirit of community/belonging to the commonwealth).

The role of employees at all levels will need to reflect intellectual discipline that demonstrates through action:

- Clear expression of ideas;
- Acceptance of personal responsibility for own thinking and managing self;
- Accepting that we and others do not know everything;
- Listening to others' views and making accurate, clear, evidenced statements; and
- Seek out knowledge and understanding: self, others, context, nature of change based on looking at reasons and discussing "why", recognising unstated assumptions and values and questioning them, analysing key components to change, and applying thinking in a critical way.

Creating bullet-point lists as above, and lists of "things to do" when discussing how to create organizational cultures that encourage participation through dialogical approaches to change is easy! The doing, however, is the difficult part as success depends on employee engagement and not just the use and reliance on rhetoric. The degree of employee engagement, as emphasised throughout this discussion, will be dependent on self-interest and how individuals interpret it relative to organizational norms and in terms of the impact of proposed change. This is the most difficult part to attempt to manage and must be seen as, to use a journey metaphor, a never-ending one that will require resilient managers whom are fully supported in the endeavours.

To conclude, the ultimate aim is one of encouraging and facilitating thinking on the part of all employees that is critical in order to address politicised conformance, and doing so based on individuals moving beyond conceptualising their role in relation to self and change, to one that is more evaluative, reflective, reasoned and goes beyond subjective concerns. This, of course, is a very tall mountain to climb, with the reality of trying to achieve such a utopian organizational climate being very difficult, as the extent to which self-interest is rooted in individuals is deep, and manifests itself in different ways and at different points in time: self-interest agenda are fluid. The degree to which managers can manage their own and others' self-interest fluidity is part of the reality of the difficulty of all of this; there is a need to be clear, realistic, as to what can actually is achievable and what is not. There is, however, a partial suggested answer to this. If the creation of a meaningful commonwealth is achieved then individuals' participation in a more open and de-politicised sense will enable managers to manage in a less politicised way: a new more open symbiotic relationship will be created, though not a necessarily a perfect one, but one that brings forth more meaningful dialogue and action.

A commonwealth of interest, however, can only be created if individuals realign self-interest based on benefits being received through organizational commonwealth, in that individual-collective self-interest is a prime motivator, whether generally and/or through change. Employees own their inner-self and therefore their behaviour. If employees are to participate in change beyond any form of notional participative approaches embedded within a linear approach, then employees need to be encouraged to find their authentic voice; a voice that is free of political sensitivities and replication of organizational rhetoric. Organizations need to be action oriented with regard to facilitating participation at a deeper level, and done so through more open management styles. This has implications for how organizations select managers and/or promote individuals into line management positions, and for leadership. Managers at the strategic apex also have a crucial role to play in setting tone through actions; simply relying on rhetoric and assuming everyone else gets the message and/or making any assumptions about the power they have is not enough. New forms of management and leadership are required; "new" in the sense of how management and leadership is demonstrated through action in order to reframe the purpose and function of management alongside leadership, generally, and in relation to managing change.

The central theme of this book has been to challenge the extent to which organizations understand the implications of self-interest, politicised conformance and change, and the preparedness of organizations to take a fresh look at the power inherent within self-interest and the degree to which it shapes behaviour and relationships at work. It has also challenged the extent to which dialogical approaches, as currently practised, get to grips with self-interested politicised conformance and the extent to which it creates the delusion of its efficacy. This, as discussed in this chapter, challenges organizations to move away from rhetoric and the assumption that it has sufficient force in itself to affect change. In this respect, there needs to be a higher degree of realism and honesty on the part of organizations. Concomitant to this, organizations need to be prepared to deform hierarchies in order to shape culture and power relationships in order to foster more open and deeper discourse, and do so based on managerial competency and relational depth (Brewis, 1996). Unless organizations radically change the constraints and control mechanisms of their holding environments, the constructs that maintain hierarchy and social order remain, thus working against the creation of a commonwealth based on reduced, not absent, levels of self-interest. Otherwise, organizations create an illusion of change through dialogue, and do so with emotive and symbolic words in order to create a narrative of change that is not only unrecognised by employees, but one that is partially ignored within the bounds of political conformity.

Again, and to refer once more to Bénabou (2009), a form of organizational delusion becomes part of the narrative. The consequences of this delusion are multi-faceted and often result in the creation of multiple realities relative to self that conflict with espoused organizational reality, the reality of which in itself reinforces politicised conformance, that brings about change irrespective of the approach used. Therefore, and as stated at the beginning of this book: *if senior management decides that change is required then irrespective of the approach used, change will happen!* My hope is that this will act as a provocative call to arms that encourages challenge through action and not just repetition of well-worn platitudes.

References

Baum, H. S. (1989) Organizational Politics Against Organizational Culture: A Psychoanalytic Perspective. *Human Resource Management*, 28(2), 191–206.

Bénabou, R. (2009*) Groupthink: Collective Delusions in Organizations and Markets*. NBER Working Paper No. 14764. Retrieved January 2012 from Princeton University website: http://static-71, 166–250.

Besharov, M. L. and Smith, W. K. (2014) Multiple Institutional Logics in Organization: Explaining Their Varied Nature and Implication. *Academy of Management Review*, 39(3), 364–381

Boje, D. (2012) Reflections: What Does Quantum Physics of Storytelling Mean for Change Management? *Journal of Change Management*, 12(3), 253–271.

Brewis, J. (1996) The Making of the "Competent" Manager Competency Development, Personal Effectiveness and Foucault. *Management Learning*, 27(1), 65–86.

Burgoyne, J., Hirsh, W. and Williams, S. (2004) *The Development of Management and Leadership Capability and Its Contribution to Performance: The Evidence, the Prospects and the Research Need*. Research Report RR560. Retrieved March 2012 from Department for Education and Skills website: www.education.gov.uk/publications/eOrderingDownload/RR560.pdf

Calhoun, C. (2001) *Putting Emotions in their Place*. In J. Goodwin et al. (eds.), *Passionate Politics: Emotions and Social Movements*. Chicago and London: University of Chicago Press.

Christiansen, N., Villanova, P. and Mikulay, S. (1997) Political Influence Compatibility: Fitting the Person to the Climate. *Journal of Organizational Behavior*, 18(6), 709–730.

Delbridge, R. and Edwards, T. (2013) Inhabiting Institution: Critical Realist Refinements to Understanding Institutional Complexity and Change. *Organization Studies*, 34(7), 927–947.

Friedland, R. and Alford, R. R. (1991) Bringing Society Back In: Symbols, Practices and Institutional Contradiction. In W. W. Powell and P. J. Di Maggio (eds.), *The New Institutionalism in Organizational Analysis*. Chicago and London: The University of Chicago Press, 232–263.

Golsorkhi, D., Courpasson, D. and Sallaz, J. (eds) (2012) Rethinking Power in Organizations, Institutions, and Markets. *Research in the Sociology of Organizations*, 34, 21–54.

Gould, L. J., Stapely, L. F. and Stein, M. (2006) *The Sytems Psychodynamics of Organizations: Integrating the Group Relations Approach, Psychoanalytical and Open Systems Perspectives* (2nd ed.). London: H. Kranac (Books) Ltd.

Greenwood, R. et al. (2010) The Multiplicity of Institutional Logics and the Heterogeneity of Organizational Responses. *Organization Science*, 21(2), 521–539.

Hannan, M. T. and Freeman, J. (1984) Structural Inertia and Organizational Change. *American Sociological Review*, 49, 149–164.

Hesson, M. and Olpin, M. (2013) *Stress Management for Life: A Research Based Experiential Approach* (3rd ed.). Andover: Cengage Learning

Hobbes, T. (1651) *Leviathan*. Reprint, London: Penguin Classics, 2017.

Kelly, D. and Amburgey, T. (1991) Organizational Inertia and Momentum: A Dynamic Model of Strategic Change. *The Academy of Management Journal*, 34(3), 591–612.

Kouzes, J. M. and Posner, B. Z. (2007) *The Leadership Challenge* (4th ed.). San Francisco: John Wiley and Sons, Inc.

Lukes, S. (1974) *Power: A Radical View*. New York: Macmillan Press.

McGuire, D. and Hutchings, K. (2006) A Machiavellian Analysis of Organizational Change. *Journal of Organizational Change Management*, 19(2), 192–209

Meyer, J. W. and Rowan, B. (1977) Institutionalised Organization: Formal Structure as Myth and Ceremony. *American Journal of Sociology*, 83(20), 340–363.

Mill, J. S. (1859) *On Liberty*. Reprint, Los Angeles: Enhanced Media Publishing, 2016.

Morgan, G. (2006) *Images of Organization*. Thousand Oaks: Sage Publications, Inc.

Oswick, C., and Jones, P. (2006) Beyond Compare? Metaphor in Organization Theory. *Academy of Management Review*, 31, 483–485.

Reed, M. (2005) Reflections on the "Realist Turn" in Organization and Management Studies. *Journal of Management Studies*, 42(8), 1621–1644.

Seddon, J. (2005) *Freedom From Command and Control: Rethinking Management for Lean Service*. Buckingham: Productivity Press.

Sheard, G., Kakabadse, A. P. and Kakabadse, N. K. (2011) Organizational Politics: Reconciling Leadership's Rational-Emotional Paradox. *Leadership and Organizational, Development Journal*, 32(1), 78–97.

Smets, M. and Jarzabkowski, P. (2013) Reconstructing Institutional Complexity in Practice: A Relational Model of Institutional Work and Complexity. *Human Relations*, 66(10), 1279–1309.

Stapley, L. F. (1996) *The Personality of the Organization: A Psycho-Dynamic Explanation of Culture and Change*. London and New York: Free Association Books.

Tilesik, A. (2010) From Ritual to Reality: Demography, Ideology, and Decoupling in a Post-Communist Government Agency. *Academy of Management Journal*, 53(6), 922–953.

Toubiana, M. and Zietsma, C. (2017) The Message is on the Wall? Emotions, Social Media and the Dynamics of Institutional Complexity. *Academy of Management Journal*, 60(3), 922–953.

Van Buskirk, W. and McGrath, D. (1999) Organizational Cultures as Holding Environments: A Psychodynamic Look at Organizational Symbolism. *Human Relations*, 52(6), 805–833.

Vigoda-Gadot, E. and Drory, A. (2006) *Handbook of Organizational Politics*. Cheltenham: Edward Elgar Publishing.

Weick, K. E. (1995) *Sensemaking in Organizations*. London: Sage Publications.

Index

Printed in the United States
by Baker & Taylor Publisher Services